The Innovator's Playbook

*Discovering and Transforming Great Ideas
Into Breakthrough New Products*

Kevin B. McGourty
"Playing the Game of Innovation to Win"

The Innovator's Playbook: Discovering and transforming great ideas into breakthrough new products

Copyright notice

The Innovator's Playbook: Discovering and Transforming Great Ideas Into Breakthrough New Products
Published by iNPD Center, Inc.
4317 St. Cloud Ct
Oakland, CA 94619
http://theinnovatorsplaybook.com

Copyright © 2015 iNPD Center, Inc.

All rights reserved. Except as permitted by applicable copyright laws, no part of this book may be reproduced, duplicated, sold or distributed in any form or by any means, either mechanical, by photocopy, electronic, or by computer, or stored in a database or retrieval system, without the express written permission of the publishers, except for brief quotations by reviewers.

ISBN: 1503387879
ISBN 13: 9781503387874

Contents

**Introduction: Do You Want To Launch
A Steady Stream Of Breakthrough New Products?.** 1

    What I've learned and will share with you 3

    How this book is organized 5

**Chapter1: Why Is It So Hard To Consistently
Innovate And Launch Successful New Products?** 9

    Did you know that 89 percent of product failures are
caused by non-technical issues?. 10

        Without clear and relevant requirements,
new product development is doomed to failure 10

    Defining requirements takes upfront effort,
resources and know-how 11

    Why not just get the product out there and
iterate to success? 12

A reliable innovation framework and
common language is now available. 12

People don't buy quarter inch drills,
they buy quarter inch holes. 13

Understanding the problem from the
customer's perspective. 14

A repeatable and predictable innovation framework . . . 15

Chapter 2: People "Hire" Products To Get Important Jobs Done 16

What are jobs? 18

Jobs-to-be-done have both functional and
emotional aspects. 19

Core jobs are stable and provide a focal point
for innovation. 21

    Products are point-in-time solutions to
    getting jobs done 22

An example of a core job: traveling from
point A to point B 22

Circumstances and constraints affect
how jobs get done 23

The goal of innovation is to help customers
get their jobs done better 24

Core concept: focus on core jobs people want done. . . . 25

Exercise: What important jobs do your
products solve? 25

**Chapter 3: Desired Outcomes Define
Customers' Success Metrics** **26**

    Desired and undesired outcomes are
the guideposts to innovation. 26

    Defining the job-map. 27

    Success is defined at each step in a job map 29

    Core concept - capturing customers' needs and
requirements is hard work. 30

    Exercise: Create a job map of an important
job you need to get done daily 30

**Chapter 4: What Prevents Customers From
Getting Jobs Done?** **31**

    Overcoming constraints can spark innovation. 32

    Constraints and barriers that prevent
non-consumers from hiring a solution. 33

    Understanding constraints and barriers
provides critical insights 35

    Exercise: What barriers prevent
non-consumption of your products?. 36

Chapter 5: The Anatomy Of A Customer's Job **37**

    Constructing a job statement to focus innovation 38

        Job statement construct: 38

        A job construct for this job scenario 38

    Primary jobs, job trees, and job chains. 39

    All jobs are processes 41

Opportunities for innovation are found
up and down a job tree 41

**Chapter 6: Creating Job Maps To Gain Insights
Into Customer Pain Points** 42

Mapping steps in a job 42

The Plan, Do, Check and Act (PDCA) continuous
improvement loop applied to job mapping 43

People do jobs to achieve desired outcomes 44

Think in terms of the purpose for the process,
not the process itself 44

Job maps provide a comprehensive framework to
identify the metrics customers use to describe success . . 45

Core concept 45

Exercise: Create a job map for an
important business activity. 46

**Chapter 7: Defining the customer's success
metrics at every step of a job** 47

How to construct an outcome statement 48

Structure provides a consistent definition
and measurement of job success. 49

Tip: Be like Columbo - keep an open mind 51

**Chapter 8: Underserved And Overserved
Outcomes Provide Guideposts to Innovate Around.** 52

Using quantitative research to Analyze outcome
statements 53

Ranking the outcomes using the
"opportunity algorithm" 53

The opportunity index provides a focal point for
innovation. 55

Determining the innovation sweet spot 55

Go where the opportunity bands point us 57

Final thoughts. 59

**Chapter 9: To Innovate Take Off Your
Product-Oriented Blinders** **61**

Ford once upon a time really was number one 62

Using a reverse jobs-to-be-done marketing lens to
change from a product to a jobs orientation 62

An example of using a reverse jobs-to-be-done
marketing lens to spot new opportunities 63

Exercise: Why do people hire your
products and services? 64

**Chapter 10: A Great Idea? Or A Solution
Looking For A Problem?** **66**

Defining value from the customer's perspective 67

An example of using the reverse
jobs-to-be-done marketing lens. 68

Exercise: Apply the reverse jobs-to-be-done
lens on a promising technology 72

**Chapter 11: Market Segmentation Using
The Jobs-To-Be-Done Marketing Lens** **73**

Overreliance on demographic or geographic
segmentation schemas. 74

What segmentation schemas should we use
to segment the market? 75

    Common market segmentation schemas 76

Viewing segmentation from the
customer's perspective 77

Final words from Yankelovich on market
segmentation strategy: 77

Exercise: Come up with a segmentation
strategy using jobs-to-be-done marketing lens 78

Chapter 12: The ABC's of Conducting Jobs-To-Be-Done Market Research 79

Using qualitative and quantitative research
techniques to uncover desired outcomes 80

Adding structure to our research 80

A good anchor question to use: 81

High and low scores provide trend information 81

Quantifying job and outcome importance
and satisfaction levels 82

Transforming raw unstructured data
into quantifiable data 82

Structuring an outcome statement 83

    Outcome statement example 1: 84

    Outcome statement example 2: 84

Chapter 13: Tips On Managing And Conducting Customer Interviews 86

Manage your interview time 86

A note about interview transcripts 87

The research team 89

What if we don't cover all the questions? 90

Wrapping up the interview 91

Chapter 14: Identifying Research Subjects 92

Finding the right job executors and
stakeholders for our research 92

Qualifying your research subjects 94

Customer visit matrix. 94

What's next in our jobs-to-be-done investigation? 95

Exercise: Validating and honing
Teknovantage's core business hypothesis 96

**Chapter 15: The Innovator's Playbook For
Predictable and Sustainable Growth. 98**

What is the innovator's playbook? 99

How to design a winning innovator's playbook 100

Defining the playing field where we'll win
customers and beat competitors 101

Playing the game of innovation. 103

Football as a metaphor 104

The skills of the game 105

The "first down" markers and goal line for
the innovation team. 106

The game of innovation is not really linear 106

The balancing act between desirability, feasibility and viability separates winners from losers. 108

The "3" criteria of design success 109

The business model canvas as a planning tool. 111

Play to win by thinking strategically and
planning your strategy time horizons. 113

    Using Strategic Time Horizons to define a
    balanced portfolio and game plan 113

    Use Strategic Buckets to achieve balance
    between risk and reward 115

    Managing in the zone 116

    Exercise: Create a business model canvas. 117

Chapter 16: Final Thoughts: **118**

    The take away about jobs-to-be-done 119

    The Innovator's Playbook to playing
    the game of innovation to win. 120

Suggested Reading List. **123**

About the Author - Kevin B. McGourty. **125**

INTRODUCTION

Do You Want To Launch A Steady Stream Of Breakthrough New Products?

INTRODUCING A STEADY stream of innovative products is the lifeblood of your organization. But if your company is like many of those I work with, all that seems to come out of your new product development efforts are undifferentiated "me-too" products, or "solutions-looking-for-problems" the market simply doesn't value or want.

When I started my career as an electronic engineer in Silicon Valley in the early 80s, product development, though certainly challenging, seemed to be a simple and straightforward process: start with a promising idea, create a specification, set the development team loose, and 12 to 18 months later, customers will beat a path to your door.

It was never quite that easy, but during the 80s and 90s, the tech industry was growing by leaps and bounds. A tech and sales orientation to product development was sufficient to win. But something changed, and changed dramatically.

What changed was the world became a more competitive playing field. With hyper global competition, and information and communications that move at the speed of lightning, the environment changed from complicated to complex. Today technology is copied quickly, and rapidly becomes a commodity. Competitors from around the world copy our products relentlessly.

As a result, we start competing on specmanship, incremental improvements and lower prices, hoping we can withstand the onslaught from our competitors by running faster and offering cheaper prices. What we get are me-too products that customers can't differentiate from one another, and competition becomes a bloody war of one-upmanship and price.

Customers' attitudes and expectations evolved as well. Customers expect more from their products than basic functionality. They want to be wowed and delighted by the total experience a company delivers to them. With all the choices available to them, they have very little tolerance for poor design and poor customer service.

But how do we really know what will delight our customers? How can we identify true needs that customers themselves may not recognize? When we ask customers directly what they want, all they can come up with are incremental improvements to what they already do and know. As Henry Ford famously said about a customer's ability to provide innovative ideas:

"If I had asked people what they wanted,
they would have said faster horses."

What I've learned and will share with you

Over the years, I've had my share of successes and failures in launching new products. I asked myself:

- Why were some of my products huge successes while others were total flops?
- How can I get better at discovering great ideas and transforming them into winning new products more consistently?
- How can I focus on the best opportunities while having the means and courage to discard marginal ideas?

Thus began my career journey to discover, understand and codify a body of knowledge that'll provide you with a simple, repeatable and predictable innovation process. It takes the uncertainty and risk out of discovering great ideas and transforming them into successful new products.

What resulted is a process based on the "Jobs-To-Be-Done" (J2BD) innovation theory. Jobs-to-be-done is an innovation framework pioneered by Clayton Christensen from the Harvard Business School[1], Anthony Ulwick[2] from Strategyn, and my own hands-on application of the theory with clients.

The core concept behind the jobs-to-be-done innovation framework is that people want to "hire" a product to do a job, or, as Harvard Business School marketing professor Theodore

---

[1] **Clayton M. Christensen** is the Kim B. Clark Professor of Business Administration at the Harvard Business School (HBS). He is best known for his study of innovation in commercial enterprises

[2] **Anthony (Tony) W. Ulwick** is the founder and Chief Executive Officer of Strategyn, LLC. an innovation consulting firm based in San Francisco. He is the creator of Outcome-Driven Innovation (ODI).

Levitt[3] put it, *"People don't want quarter-inch bits. They want quarter-inch holes."*

In his Harvard Business Review (HBR) article, "Marketing Malpractice: The Cause and the Cure,"[4] Clayton Christensen argues that the marketer's task is to understand the job the customer wants to get done, and design products and brands that fill that need. When people find themselves with a job to get done, they hire products to do that job for them.

The framework you're about to learn provides a systematic approach to understanding customer needs upfront. It takes you step-by-step through a simple and repeatable innovation process that focuses on the important jobs customers are trying to get done, and the outcomes they want to accomplish by doing those jobs. It takes into account the circumstances, challenges, and obstacles that are preventing them from achieving 100 percent satisfaction.

When you complete this playbook, **you'll have an innovation framework to guide you in carrying out the necessary upfront discovery and vetting activities to identify problems worth solving.** You'll learn how to transform initial concepts into solutions that customers want and value. You can expect a steady stream of successful new product introductions while avoiding the frustration and waste of launching product duds.

---

3 **Theodore Levitt** was an American economist and professor at the Harvard Business School. In his book " The Marketing Imagination" (1983,1986 – The Free Press) he introduces us to the now famous quote: *"People don't want quarter-inch bits. They want quarter-inch holes."*

4 **"Marketing Malpractice: The Cause and the Cure."** Clayton M. Christensen, Scott Cook, and Taddy Hall. Harvard Business Review December 2005

How this book is organized

In Chapter 1 we explore the challenges of launching successful new products. We examine the root causes behind new product development failures. We then introduce the jobs-to-be-done innovation framework as a repeatable front end innovation process that can improve success rates dramatically.

In Chapter 2 we define a job as a task, objective or goal a person or organization is trying to accomplish, or a problem they are trying to solve. Core jobs are both important and essential if people are to achieve significant goals in their daily lives.

In Chapter 3 we learn that when people execute jobs (the job executors), they have specific desired outcomes and results in mind. Job success and satisfaction, from the customer's perspective, is measured by defining the customer's needs and achieving those outcomes.

In Chapter 4 we examine how circumstances, constraints and barriers define the context and challenges customers face in executing their jobs and achieving 100 percent satisfaction. Understanding the job executor's context is the third core concept of the jobs-to-be-done innovation framework.

In Chapters 5, 6, and 7 we dive deeper into the nuts and bolts of the jobs-to-be-done innovation methodology. We learn how to define jobs and outcome statements, and how to create job maps using the Plan, Do, Check, and Act (PDCA) continuous improvement loop as a starting point to break down the steps involved in executing a job or a chain of jobs.

In Chapter 8 we analyze outcome statements using quantitative research. Up to this point, much of our market research was discovery based and qualitative. In Chapters 6 and 7 we discovered that a typical job chain will have anywhere between 50 to more than 150[5] outcome statements depending on the complexity of the job-to-be-done.

Then we introduce the opportunity index[6], a systematic method to rank and prioritize the desired outcomes with the highest impact in defining solutions customers will embrace and choose over alternative competing solutions. If an outcome is important and unsatisfied, it's a good indication of an innovation area to explore and exploit.

In Chapter 9 we see how to go from a product to a jobs oriented view by refocusing on why customers hire our products in the first place. Questions we can ask to focus on the job executor's (customer's) perspective are:

- What jobs are people trying to get done by hiring our products?
- What are the ultimate outcomes they are trying to achieve by doing these jobs?
- Is this the primary job they're trying to get done or is it one step in a chain of jobs?
- What circumstances and constraints do they face in executing their jobs?
- From their perspective, how satisfied are they with the outcomes they are currently achieving?

In Chapter 10 we learn how to use the jobs-to-be-done marketing lens in reverse order to define which potential and real

---

5 "What Customers Want," Anthony W. Ulwick, The McGraw-Hill Companies, 2005, chapter 2, page 27.
6 "What Customers Want," Anthony W. Ulwick, The McGraw-Hill Companies, 2005, chapter 3 page 45.

jobs people are trying to get done, where our solution becomes the obvious choice for hire.

In Chapter11 we study how to use the jobs-to-be-done innovation framework to segment the market. Defining market segments is one of the most critical decisions a company makes in planning its overall strategy to achieve its growth goals.

In Chapter 12 we inquire into using quantitative questions such as: "On a scale of 1 to 10, what level of satisfaction are you achieving in getting your job done?" We also learn how to use follow-up qualitative question such as: "Why did you give it that score?" and: "What would it take to make it a 10?" Probing with qualitative questions provides real insights into what customers want.

In Chapters 13 and 14 we provide guidelines on how to plan, organize and conduct market research interviews. For a 60-minute interview, we should have 10 to 15 anchor questions to facilitate the conversation. Valuable information comes when we probe deeper into a subject's story, allowing him or her to share experiences of getting jobs done.

We determine how to find and qualify the right research subjects, and how to approach them. We look at how to get organized by creating a customer visit matrix that lists who we plan to call, for what purpose (interviewee and/or referral) and their basic demographics (job executor, expert, supervisor, buyer, channel member, etc.) Then we emphasize the importance of creating a good contact script that helps us communicate clearly and precisely, and engage our subjects.

In Chapter 15 we present **the innovator's playbook to discovering problems worth solving and creating solutions customers will hire.** The first step in the innovator's playbook is setting a direction based on the current jobs-for-hire solutions a company is providing for existing job executors (customers), modifying existing job solutions to address new job executors, addressing new jobs solutions for existing customers, and the most challenging and potentially rewarding play in the book, addressing new jobs for new job executors.

We then discuss the game of innovation and new product development. It's the game of moving through the knowledge funnel starting from an initial hunch (idea), to a heuristic (early market success), to an algorithm (mainstream market success).

For the innovation team to win consistently, it needs to become skilled at executing an innovation system like the jobs-to-be-done framework. The team must master the discovery process, the design and development process, the manufacturing process and/or the service creation process, and the marketing and sales process to launch and scale the business.

CHAPTER 1

Why Is It So Hard To Consistently Innovate And Launch Successful New Products?

EVEN WITH AN abundance of innovation literature and know-how, success rates for new products is disappointingly low. According to Clayton Christensen, at the Harvard Business School and author of "*The Innovator's Solution*:[7]"

"Over 60 percent of all new product development efforts are scuttled before they ever reach the market. Of the 40 percent that do see the light of day, 40 percent fail to become profitable and are withdrawn from the market. By the time you add it all up, three-quarters of the

---
7 "The Innovator's Solution: Creating and Sustaining Successful Growth," Clayton Christensen and Michael Raynor, Harvard Business Review Press, 2003

money spent in product development investments results in products that do not succeed commercially."

Did you know that 89 percent of product failures are caused by non-technical issues?

According to Dr. Robert Cooper[8], a recognized thought leader in new product development, only 11 percent of product development failures are for technical reasons associated with the performance of the product itself. The predominant causes of new product failure are marketing or market-related reasons. These include developing products the customer did not want and developing me-too products.

Without clear and relevant requirements, new product development is doomed to failure

All too often, development teams march forward to launch without a clear understanding of customer requirements (what customers need and desire), thinking they know what's best for the customer. Companies make too many assumptions in the definition phase and base product requirements on opinions, not market realities. As a result, they end up launching me-too products and solutions-looking-for-problems customers neither value or want.

Or perhaps the development team thinks it's getting the right data by asking customers what they want. But customers may be too close to "just getting their jobs done today" the way they've always done them. Thus they are unable or unaware of how to imagine, let alone articulate, new approaches to get their important jobs done better.

---

8 Winning at New Products: Creating Value Through Innovation, Robert G. Cooper, Basic Books; 4 edition, July 12, 2011

Defining requirements takes upfront effort, resources and know-how

There are several reasons why development teams don't invest enough time to understand the customer's problem set up front. Some development teams have been successful in the past by using their own instincts and assumptions of what the market wants. They believe what worked in the past will work in the future.

Sometimes this works, especially in the hyper growth stage of a technology adoption curve (i.e. inside the tornado[9]) where customers will accept less than perfect solutions to keep pace with the new paradigm (enabled by a new technology/process/business model) so as not to be left behind.

But tornados are rare, and customers have become a lot more sophisticated when it comes to adopting new technologies. Customers want products and services that give them total solutions that result in complete satisfaction and delight.

Quite often, technology evolves along clear and predictable performance vectors (e.g. microprocessor clock rates) that customers value. Companies can be very successful in creating product roadmaps around these performance vectors. Clayton Christensen calls this "sustainable innovation.[10]" Eventually performance vectors overshoot the market and investing more development resources results in diminishing returns.

Or worse, a disruptive solution comes along redefining the market (e.g. mobile computing and the personal computer).

---

[9] Inside the Tornado: Strategies for Developing, Leveraging, and Surviving Hypergrowth Markets, Geoffrey A. Moore, Collins Business Essentials, (2004). Inside the tornado refers to a hyper growth period in the market adoption lifecycle.

[10] The Innovator's Dilemma: When New Technologies Cause Great Firms to Fail, Clayton M. Christensen, Harvard Business Review Press, 2000

The performance vectors we put so much development effort into yesterday, no longer matter in this new market reality – we missed the boat and now we have to play catch-up.

Why not just get the product out there and iterate to success?

Some developers believe time is better served by just getting a product out there and learning quickly. This approach can work. In some industries like software, a build, test and iterate approach provides a path to co-develop solutions with early adopter customers.

The philosophy of iterative methods is to create a "minimally viable product"[11] as fast as possible and work with paying customers to identify and validate an expanded set of requirements as you go. Iterative approaches work because they build on real requirements defined by the customer and are tested and validated throughout the development process.

But successful iterative development methods work more effectively and efficiently when companies understand critical requirements upfront, before a development cycle begins. Without clear direction and requirements, they can spend lots of resources and time chasing phantom problems resulting in solutions-looking-for problems.

A reliable innovation framework and common language is now available

I believe the main reason why companies don't invest time up front in uncovering and defining requirements is that they

---

11 The Lean Startup: How Today's Entrepreneurs Use Continuous Innovation to Create Radically Successful Businesses, Eric Ries, Crown Business, 2011

don't know how. They don't have a repeatable and reliable front end process that allows them to gain deep insights into the customer's problem set, and a method to translate these insights into relevant requirements they can innovate around.

Many companies also confuse specifications with requirements. They assume too early in the exploration and design process that they have THE solution for THE problem under investigation and jump into creating specifications. As a result, they end up with solutions based on prior knowledge that no longer provides a differentiated solution but rather a me-too product that forces a company to compete in a "red ocean.[12]"

People don't buy quarter inch drills, they buy quarter inch holes

In his classic book on marketing, The Marketing Imagination (1983), Theodore Levitt pointed out that when customers buy quarter inch drill bits, what they really want are quarter inch holes. It seems like an obvious distinction. Yet many businesses think of themselves as being in the business of manufacturing products versus being in the business of providing the means – through products and services – for people to solve their problems.

When companies become too product and technology focused, they run the risk of adding more features and functions to their current products because they believe that their

---

12 Red oceans refer to the known market space – all the industries in existence today. In red oceans, industry boundaries are clearly delineated and accepted, and the competitive rules of the game are known. Companies try to outperform their rivals to grab a greater share of existing demand, usually through marginal changes in offering level and price. As the market space gets crowded, prospects for profits and growth are reduced. Products become commodities, and cut-throat competition turns the red ocean bloody

customers want more and better of the same thing. When companies do this, they often solve the wrong problems: they improve their products in ways that are irrelevant to their customers' needs. The result is either undifferentiated me-too products or solutions-looking-for–a-problem.

Understanding the problem from the customer's perspective

The jobs-to-be-done innovation framework provides a clear understanding of important jobs (i.e. goals, task and solving problems) people face, their circumstance and challenges in executing the job, and how people define success of completing a job in their terms.

By exploring and answering the following questions, the development team will have the right set of market insights to develop clear and relevant requirements:

1. What jobs are people trying to get done and why?
2. What are the desired outcomes people are trying to accomplish by doing the job?
3. What circumstances and constraints do they face in getting these jobs done?
4. How satisfied are they with the desired outcomes (results) they are getting?

It's up to us as developers to understand what important jobs customers are trying to get done. Our target customers are the experts in executing their current jobs. Customers may or may not know HOW to get their jobs done better, but they will know WHY they are doing the jobs in the first place, and what desired outcomes they are trying to achieve.

A repeatable and predictable innovation framework

The jobs-to-be-done innovation framework provides a repeatable and predictable method of discovering problems worth solving and defining the right set of product requirements to innovate around.

It reduces the guesswork and uncertainty associated with the innovation process by providing a systematic approach to discovering what important jobs customers need to get done, how customers define success by expressing their desired outcomes, and what prevents them from achieving 100 percent satisfaction.

CHAPTER 2

People "Hire" Products To Get Important Jobs Done

PEOPLE DON'T BUY products. They "hire" products to solve important problems. Think about the last time you bought a product, maybe new software or an app for your smart phone. What were the factors that drove you to make the decision to buy the product?

Chances are you were actively looking for a product to solve a problem you were having. Or, when the product presented itself to you (i.e. you found it somewhat serendipitously), it clarified a problem (or desire) you may not have been totally aware of, and it motivated you to take action to hire it.

The concept of understanding jobs-to-be-done was articulated by Clayton Christensen in his must read book *"The*

Innovator's Solution.: Creating and Sustaining Successful Growth[13]." Here's what Christensen says about jobs-to-be-done:

*"When customers become aware of a job that they need to get done in their lives, they look around for a product or service **that they can "hire" to get the job done.**"*

For example, recently I remodeled my bathroom. The first job on the list was to upgrade the bathroom floor. I wanted to hire a floor product that I could easily install by myself, would be affordable and would look great when the job was completed.

It turned out there were lots of products I could hire to get the job done. They ranged from the most inexpensive linoleum (but that's what I wanted to replace) to stone and ceramic tile, which looked fantastic. However it looked too involved to install given my skill level, time, existing tools, and desire to take on that big of a job.

After researching on the web and visiting my local favorite home improvements stores, I hired a stone laminate product that looked great in the show room, appeared very simple to install, and was priced at a point that made hiring the product the obvious choice to get my job done.

Though the process was not hassle-free, I'm happy to say I'm delighted with the results I achieved in executing my job. The floor looks great – but not perfect (perhaps that's my inner critic coming to the surface!)

In executing my job, I discovered there were many other sub-jobs that needed to be done. I needed to hire more tools

---

13 "The Innovator's Solution: Creating and Sustaining Successful Growth," Clayton Christensen and Michael Raynor, Harvard Business Review Press, 2003

(products) to execute these jobs. I love tools, so this was a nice way to justify adding to my tool collection - at least that's what I told my wife!

I share this story of a real situation to explain the jobs-to-be-done innovation framework. Along the spectrum of complicated jobs, installing a floor is somewhere in the middle between trivial to heroic – but it's a good example of the jobs-to-be-done innovation framework.

What are jobs?

Let's begin by creating a definition of a job:

- **A job is a task, objective or goal a person or organization is trying to accomplish or a problem they are trying to solve.**

    In my case the problem I wanted to solve was to improve the appearance of my bathroom by upgrading the floor.

- **The job is important to them and they are dedicated to getting the job done.**

    For my wife and me, it's important that our house looks great. It's our castle and our pride and joy. Upgrading the bathroom is just one job to be done in achieving our goal.

- **Customers migrate to products that get the job done best, according to their definition of success (desired outcomes).**

The laminated stone floor fit my bill. The product looks great. It was relatively easy to install. It was affordable and easy to purchase. For the most part, it satisfied my desired outcomes in doing the job. We will talk more about desired outcomes in Chapter 3.

Jobs-to-be-done have both functional and emotional aspects

A functional job describes the task that a job executor wants to accomplish. In my case, this was upgrading and installing a new bathroom floor to improve the look and quality of my bathroom.

There's also a higher level job **(core functional job)** I want done: making improvements to my house to achieve my desired outcome of having a great looking and comfortable home. Upgrading the floor is just one node in the overall home improvement job tree. (We explore job trees in chapter 3.)

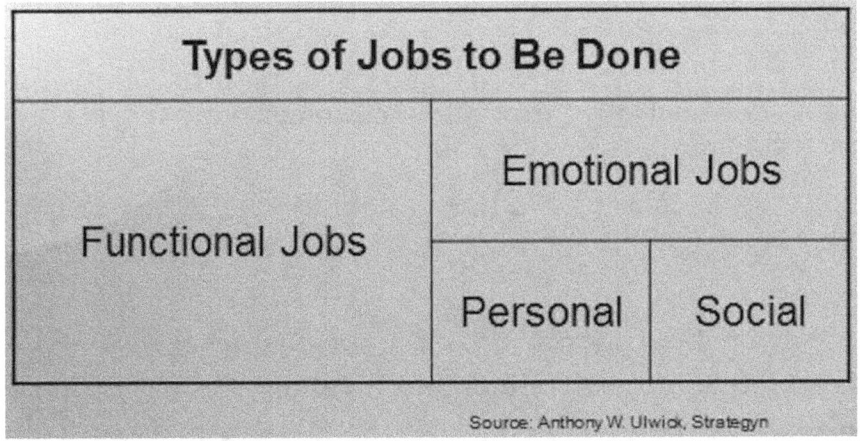

Figure 2.1: Jobs have functional and emotional aspects

The functional dimensions of the job are the steps a job executor takes to define, plan, prepare, execute and conclude a job. These steps are called the job map. A job map provides a visual depiction of the job deconstructed into discrete process steps, and explaining in detail what the job executor is trying to get done.

With a job map in place, we can capture the desired outcomes of the job executor for each step in the job map. We innovate around these core elements by understanding the desired outcomes.

In my example, the functional job included all the steps I took from initially defining what my bathroom improvement project would entail, how I'd get it done, what products I'd hire and gather to get the job done, the actual job execution, and finally concluding the job by cleaning up my job site. Completing the job and feeling great about the final outcome brings us to the emotional dimensions of jobs-to-be-done.

Emotional jobs are related to feelings and perceptions, and as such they are subjective. There are two kinds of emotional jobs:

- Personal jobs describe how customers want to feel about themselves.
- Social jobs refer to how customers want to be perceived by others.

For my flooring project, **on a personal level I** wanted to feel good about my abilities and my skill in using my hands to create a beautiful floor. Had the floor turned out badly, my emotional job would have been underserved and I'd have been left feeling bad about myself. As it is now, I feel pretty darn good about myself. I created a great result with my own hands!

On a social level, I'm very proud to show off my handy work to friends and visitors. I'm tickled pink when they say to me: "Wow, you did that by yourself!" They think of me as a very talented handyman and craftsman and that's an important persona I like to project out to the world.

Core jobs are stable and provide a focal point for innovation

A salient concept of jobs-to-be-done innovation theory is that core jobs are stable over time. These jobs are both important and essential for people to conduct their daily lives and achieve important goals.

Core jobs don't fundamentally change that much. What changes is HOW to get the job done. This is often enabled by technology.

Core jobs are the fundamental problems customers want solved. They are the higher purpose for which customers hire products, services and solutions. A core job may be an end in itself (primary job) or a means to an end for a higher level job. We explore primary jobs in greater detail in chapter 5.

For example, a person's primary job may be to stock his kitchen with food to feed his family for a week. So he decides to go grocery shopping at the local market. To execute his primary job, he must travel from his home (point A) to the store (point B), do his shopping, and return with his groceries.

Going from point A to point B and back is an important job he needs to execute and he will hire a solution to get his job done. But stocking food in his kitchen is the primary job he seeks to get done. What other ways might he execute this important job?

Products are point-in-time solutions to getting jobs done

With this perspective, it becomes clear that products are point-in-time solutions that enable customers to get jobs done. For example, people need to travel for various reasons, but the fundamental job is to go physically from point A to point B.

An example of a core job: traveling from point A to point B

In the very beginning people had only one or two options: they could either walk from point A to point B, or be carried by someone else.

Along came the domesticated horse and the wheel, enabling a new and better way to travel farther, faster, and easier. And for some people, boats gave them an alternative new way of traveling better. In some circumstances, boats and horse drawn carriages competed for the same customers, whose job was to travel from point A to point B.

The wheel and the domesticated horse brought more jobs to be done: creating wagons, carriages, saddles, as well as livery stables, barns, etc. An ecosystem of industries evolved over time to address the fundamental job of travel. And the same development applied to boats and ships.

Next came the steam engine creating a new possibility for passenger transportation in the form of railroads and steam-powered ships. Again a new ecosystem and new jobs-to-be-done developed to support the core job of travel. In fact, the railroad made travel so much better and easier, it enabled a whole new economic boom and expansion.

Continuing along the evolution of powered engines, the internal combustion engine was next. It resulted in the creation of horseless carriages (a.k.a. the automobile), Trains and water craft became more efficient. But they were all still addressing the fundamental job-to-be-done of passenger travel (and of course cargo – a related job but not the same).

A major breakthrough in technology created airplanes as a viable form of passenger and personal travel. It was further enabled by the evolution of the combustion engine, that was later transformed by the invention of the jet engine.

What's next in passenger travel? Rocket ships for space travel perhaps? More likely electric and/or green technology powered vehicles? Or will virtual reality replace travel? Perhaps for when travel is used to accomplish *the job of meeting face-to-face,* but probably not for the basic job of travel which I predict will continue to exist well into the future.

Circumstances and constraints affect how jobs get done

Job executors execute jobs under specific circumstances and constraints. Marketers and developers need to understand these parameters before defining a solution to help a job executor get important jobs done better. This is an important concept in jobs-to-be-done theory.

When we factor in circumstances and constraints, we improve our chances of creating a product and service that addresses "real" jobs that are currently underserved. For example, we wouldn't take a jumbo jet to go from our house down to our local grocery store (circumstances don't make air travel feasible, at least not with a jumbo jet!) Nor would we take our car to travel from San Francisco to Tokyo (circumstance and constraint of traveling across the Pacific Ocean).

In Chapter 4, we'll explore in greater detail how circumstances and constraints factor into jobs-to-be-done innovation theory.

The goal of innovation is to help customers get their jobs done better

From our example, we can see that while technology and social adoption changed the way people travel, it didn't change the core job of why people travel – to go from point A to point B. Instead technology and innovation enabled people to get the core job of travel done better.

Technology and innovation also opened up new possibilities of travel, both in time and space, that otherwise would never have been possible. And each new form of travel in turn created a whole new business ecosystem that supported the various industries that arose from a simple concept:

"Helping customers get their important jobs done better through innovation and new products."

Had innovators and developers focused on improving the horse and horse carriages, perhaps the automobile would never have been invented. But luckily for us, innovators like Henry Ford knew better; innovation wasn't about making horses faster, but rather, making the important job of moving people from point A to point B more effective.

At the same time, innovation addressed important desired outcomes that weren't being satisfied by horse and buggy: traveling farther in less time and more comfort, while enjoying more travel flexibility and a sense of independence (emotional job) than a horse could provide.

Core concept: focus on core jobs people want done

The core idea behind jobs-to-be-done innovation is to discover and understand what jobs people are really trying to accomplish, what desired outcomes they're trying to achieve by doing the job, under what circumstances they're trying to execute the job, and what prevents them from achieving their desired outcomes with 100 percent satisfaction.

As marketers and product developers, the better we understand up front the problems people have, and how people define success on their terms, the better our odds of creating winning new products and services. The jobs-to-be-done innovation framework provides both the structure and a common language we can use to discover and define what customers really want to achieve in executing jobs. We can innovate around this knowledge foundation.

> **Exercise:** What important jobs do your products solve?
>
> Take a look at the products and services your company currently provide. Why do people "hire" your products? What important jobs are they trying to get? What is their ultimate desired outcomes in executing their job?

CHAPTER 3

Desired Outcomes Define Customers' Success Metrics

JOB SUCCESS IS measured by the outcomes the job executor wants and expects. When someone executes a job (the job executor), he has specific outcomes and results in mind. For example, when the job involves mowing the lawn, the desired outcome is to have a well-manicured lawn that looks great.

The job executor also wants all the steps of the job to be executed as effectively possible. For example, when manicuring the lawn, the product hired, let's say a powered lawn mower, should start on the first pull, catch the cut grass automatically, and cut the lawn uniformly without scalping it.

Desired and undesired outcomes are the guideposts to innovation

If developers want to improve an existing product or to create a new product, they must figure out where the customer struggles in the execution of a specific job and then devise ways to help the customer get the job done better.

A job can be as simple as manicuring the lawn, or as complex as managing the flow of inventory and material through a manufacturing plant. Though at polar ends of complexity and financial investment, each of these jobs consists of discrete steps and decision-making points.

In the case of manicuring the lawn, the job executor hires a lawn mower with the expectation that it can get his job done perfectly under varying conditions (for example different grass heights, rugged slopes, wet conditions). Setting up the mower, fueling it, starting it, pushing and guiding it, emptying and cleaning it, and stowing it when the lawn is cut, are some of the steps involved in mowing the lawn.

Defining the job-map

These steps define the job map for one aspect of manicuring the lawn, the functional job of keeping the grass trimmed. Note: a manicured lawn is the ultimate desired outcome and represents the top of the job tree. Other jobs in this job tree include watering the lawn, trimming the edges, and weeding.

A job map provides a detailed visual map of all the steps involved in getting to a final desired result. We need to focus our innovation activities on helping a job executor get these steps done better, or even on eliminating unnecessary steps. We'll discuss job maps and job trees in greater detail in Chapter 5.

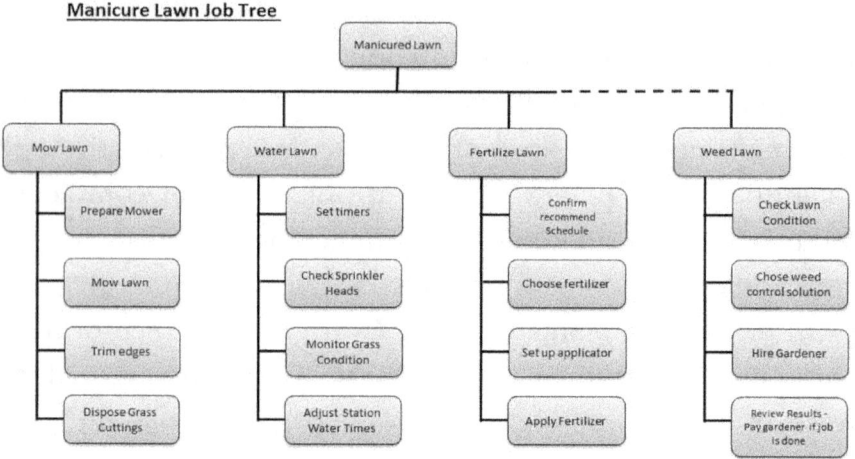

Figure 3.1: *Job map for manicuring the lawn*

The operational manager has a more complicated job: *"Managing the flow of material, parts and overall inventory to achieve maximum efficiency and throughput on her manufacturing floor and warehouse."*

She'll need to decide how much inventory she needs to carry, both in finished goods and work-in-progress, to make sure she can meet the production schedule sales has committed the company to.

She'll need an accurate sales forecast. She'll need to manage her supply chain so that it can keep up with her demands without resulting in too much inventory at the end of the year. That would result in an undesired outcome.

And she'll need to work with engineering services to make sure the documentation she uses on the factory floor reflects current release levels. She doesn't want to complete a sub-assembly only to discover it's no longer up to spec. That's another undesired outcome she wants to eliminate.

Indeed, for the operational manager, managing her manufacturing floor will involve lots of steps and sub-jobs. All these sub-jobs and job steps define the job tree and job maps of the primary job. In this case, the primary job is running a lean, efficient manufacturing operation.

The point I want to make is that jobs are processes and methods that consist of multiple steps and decision points. Each step and decision point along a job map produces outcomes that the job executor desires, or undesired outcomes the job executor wants to avoid.

Success is defined at each step in a job map

Whether we're talking about multiple jobs inside a job tree, or a standalone job, each step within a job has its own set of desired outcomes that define success. Not just the ultimate outcome, but all the steps along the way from beginning to end. Knowing desired and undesired outcomes at each step is critical. These define the customer's needs based on the functional job to be carried out, They also provide the customer's definition of "getting the job done successfully."

The real power of the jobs-to-be-done innovation approach comes from identifying and prioritizing a set of desired outcomes the customer wants to achieve in executing his job. Depending on the complexity of a job, we can expect to uncover from 50 to over 150 desired outcomes per job[14]. In Chapter 8 we'll explore how to prioritize underserved and important outcomes using the opportunity algorithm.

---

14 What Customers Want," Anthony W. Ulwick, The McGraw-Hill Companies, 2005, chapter 2, page 27.

Core concept - capturing customers' needs and requirements is hard work

Don't expect a customer to be able to precisely articulate all of his desired outcomes to you. It's not quite that easy because most customers don't think about their jobs in a structured innovation framework. It's up to us as researchers and developers to listen to our customers and observe the jobs they're trying to do. Then we can translate the raw input into actionable information.

In Chapters 12, 13 and 14, we'll explore in greater detail how to gather customer inputs, and how to translate these inputs into requirements we can innovate around. In the meantime, get out of the office, figure out what important jobs your customers really want done, and how you can help them do their jobs more easily, in less time, with less money and no hassles!

> **Exercise:** Create a job map of an important job you need to get done daily.
>
> For example planning your day's activities. Or perhaps a high level job map of developing new products.

CHAPTER 4

What Prevents Customers From Getting Jobs Done?

CIRCUMSTANCES, CONSTRAINTS AND barriers define the context and challenges customers face in executing their jobs to go from their present state of need and desire to their future state of satisfaction and delight. This is **the third core concept of the jobs-to-be-done innovation framework.**

Overcoming constraints and understanding the context a person faces in getting a job done can mean the difference between a customer being 100 percent satisfied and delighted versus being less than satisfied and looking for a better solution to hire the next time he needs to get a job done.

For example, perhaps a customer is on a business trip, traveling by car from Los Angeles to San Francisco on I5 (his context). But it's a long way to San Francisco (his constraint) and he's hungry (his circumstance).

He wants to stop and get a healthy meal, without spending too much time or money getting this job done (desired outcomes). Unfortunately all he can find are fast food chains where he'd rather not eat (undesired outcome). He reluctantly decides to make a personal sacrifice and eat a burger and fries. His hunger is satisfied but his desired outcome of eating a healthy meal is unmet. He feels bad about his decision to eat junk food.

Had there been a convenient alternative restaurant along the way, perhaps he wouldn't have made that sacrifice. Or perhaps if one of the fast food chains had a deeper understanding of travelers' desired outcomes, they'd offer a healthy meal and promote it to healthy eaters.

There may have been a very nice place just a little way off the highway where he could have gone to eat. But because he wasn't aware of it, he was unable to make that choice. Maybe if a location-based service company had done a better job of targeting the business traveler with the job-to-be-done of "eating healthy on the road," travelers would hire them regularly as a trusted recommendation source.

Overcoming constraints can spark innovation

Understanding how a new technology can overcome a specific constraint is a great strategy in defining winning solutions. For example, when Customer Relationship Management (CRM) and Sales Force Automation (SFA) software were first introduced to the market, these solutions were primarily targeted to larger enterprises.

These larger enterprises typically had the IT staff and capital resources to manage the integration, training and maintenance jobs. Small to midsize firms also wanted to improve their sales force effectiveness and better manage their customer relationships. But the customer relationship management and sales force automation solutions at the time were too complex, expensive, and time-consuming for them to learn. Smaller and midsize firms were non-customers of these solutions.

Then new technologies enabled "software as a service," now known as "cloud computing." Innovative firms like Salesforce.com and NetSuite created a solution that overcame critical constraints and barriers enabling them to reach a new segment of job executors.

Salesforce.com and NetSuite established an initial market niche, in this case small and midsize business, and gradually moved on to penetrate the larger enterprise segment. This is a great example of a disruptive business and chasm-crossing strategy.

Constraints and barriers that prevent non-consumers from hiring a solution

Non-consumers often face constraints that prevent them from hiring existing products and services. As innovators, we need to look for potential customers who are currently non-consumers (they aren't hiring solutions) because they face a barrier. If this barrier were removed, it would result in them hiring a solution to get their important job done better, faster, and cheaper.

Four core constraints limit and impede consumption

1. **Complexity** - customers find the solution too complex and believe they lack the skill set to hire the product and service, or they don't have the requisite ability to do it themselves.

2. **Cost** - the cost is too much for the customer to hire the product.
3. **Time-consuming** - it'll take too much time for the customer to justify the service. Time to learn and time to execute are some examples.
4. **Convenience** - it's not convenient enough for a customer to fire his old solution and hire a new one. It may be too inconvenient to switch out an old technology for a new one because the customer doesn't see or understand the potential pay-off.

Often disruptive solutions are born by addressing constraints with a "good enough" solution for a non-consumer group. According to disruption theory[15], the solution will improve over time and eventually become accepted by mainstream markets. Often it'll have a superior value compared to the incumbents' solutions.

---

15 Disruptive innovation, a term coined by Clayton Christensen, describes a process by which a product or service takes root initially in simple applications at the bottom of a market and then relentlessly moves up market, eventually displacing established competitors.

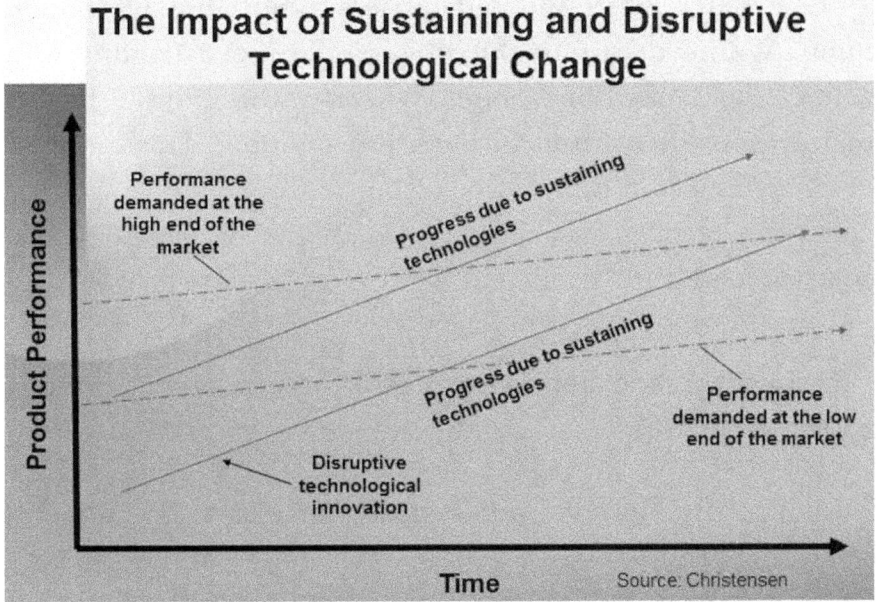

Figure 4.1: *The impact of sustaining and disruptive technology change*

Understanding constraints and barriers provides critical insights

As we apply the jobs-to-be-done innovation framework, we start asking these questions to uncover untapped opportunities:

- What prevents customers from achieving 100 percent satisfaction in getting jobs done?
- What circumstances do customers face in getting the job done?
- What constraints prevent customers from achieving 100 percent job satisfaction?
- What barriers prevent non-customers from hiring a solution?

One man's constraints and barriers is another man's opportunity. We need to find out why people are struggling with getting their jobs done better. What are the limiting factors that prevent them from hiring a job solution? This question help us discover a rich source of innovative concepts. We can create a new blue ocean[16] (see Chapter 8) in which we can compete and win.

> **Exercise:** What barriers prevent non-consumption of your products?
>
> What constraints and barriers do potential customers have which, if eliminated, would result in creating and retaining new customers?
>
> Examine the four core constraints on consumption and identify which ones, if removed, would enable non-customers to hire your solutions.

---

16 Blue Ocean Strategy – W. Chan Kim and Renée Mauborgne. Based on a study of 150 strategic moves spanning more than a hundred years and thirty industries, Kim & Mauborgne show that companies can succeed not by battling competitors, but rather by creating "blue oceans" of uncontested market space. These strategic moves create a leap in value for the company, its buyers, and its employees, while unlocking new demand and making the competition irrelevant. The book presents analytical frameworks and tools that foster an organization's ability to systematically create and capture blue oceans.

CHAPTER 5

The Anatomy Of A Customer's Job

IN CHAPTER 2 we discovered that people hire products and services to get important jobs done. We learned that a job is a task, objective or goal a person or organization is trying to accomplish, or a problem they are trying to solve.

Since the job is important to them, and they're dedicated to getting the job done, they are drawn to products that get the job done best according to their definition of success (their desired outcomes).

In this chapter we'll look at the anatomy of a customer's job and learn how to construct job statements to focus our innovation.

Constructing a job statement to focus innovation

Job statement construct:
[Customer] wants to [solve a problem] in [this circumstance]

Deconstructing the job statement into its 3 main components:

- The customer who has the job, also known as the **job executor**
- What they're trying to get done and why - **desired outcomes**
- The context in which the job occurs - **circumstances, constraints, and barriers**

For example, on construction sites a lot of time is wasted looking for tools and materials needed to execute construction jobs. The right tools aren't brought to the site, so the job executor has to go back to his shop to get them. Tools are put down and quickly lost in the clutter of the site. Or perhaps a fellow construction worker borrows a tool and doesn't return it. Or worse, he doesn't tell his fellow worker he borrowed the tool and the job executor goes on a frantic search looking for it.

A job construct for this job scenario

Construction workers want to have the right tools, equipment and materials within easy reach. They don't want to have to search for them when working on messy and cluttered work sites.

Let's take a deeper look at the job statement construct in this example.

The customer/job executor

- Construction workers.

The problem to solve

- Having the right tools on hand to do the job, to avoid going back to the tool crib or local hardware store to replace missing tools and materials.
- Losing tools on site and searching for them costs a lot of wasted time and increases job frustration.

Circumstances

- A job site located several minutes to hours away from the central tool crib and hardware store, making it time-consuming and expensive to order a replacement tool.
- Job site clutter and chaos (i.e. lots of activities going on) makes it likely a tool will get lost if not kept close by.

Primary jobs, job trees, and job chains

Having the right tools at the right time on a construction site, and keeping tabs on these tools, is an example of a sub-job or task within a larger job-to-be-done context.

A **primary job** is the fundamental problem a customer faces or the ultimate outcome he desires. For a construction job, many jobs need to be executed in order to achieve the **primary job** of erecting a building. This job is defined by his work order and schematics. Bringing the right tools and materials to the job site and keeping track of them, is a sub-job he has to do in executing the primary job.

All the sub-jobs required to execute the primary job make up what's called the **"job tree."** A job tree is a hierarchical representation of the primary job-to-be-done. We can think of jobs in terms of a **top-down-break-down structure**, similar to how project managers break down complicated tasks (i.e. work breakdown structure or WBS), and how system engineers define complicated systems (system, sub-systems, components and bills of materials).

The construction worker might have many nodes in his job tree including building a foundation, framing, roofing, dry walling, wiring, plumbing, finishing and so forth. In larger construction jobs, specialized crews are hired to carry out specific job nodes, for example carpenters, roofers, electricians and painters.

Each of the job nodes represents discrete jobs-to-be-done with its own set of sub-jobs and desired outcomes, called **"job chains,"** which define the tasks and steps required to get higher level jobs done. See Figure 5.1.

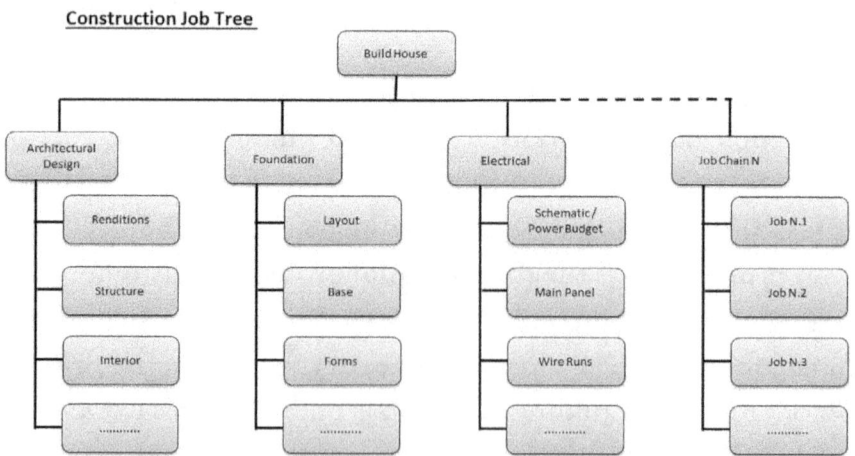

Figure 5.1: Job tree for building a house

All jobs are processes

Taking the concept of work breakdown structure one step deeper, each job or job chain in a job tree has a set of specific steps that a job executor carries out. Each of these steps has inputs, outputs and desired outcomes, and represents an opportunity for developers to innovate by creating solutions that help the job executor get the job done better.

In our construction example, a carpenter (the job executor) is tasked with the job of hanging a door (the job-to-be-done in a job chain). The carpenter plans his work by referring to his job order and schematics (job definition). He gathers and locates materials and tools to perform his job (preparation), hangs the door (job execution), makes sure the door is functioning (verifying), makes modifications if necessary (correcting), and concludes the job when the job foreman checks off the work as completed.

Opportunities for innovation are found up and down a job tree

From an innovation opportunity perspective, we can focus on jobs-to-be-done from any part of the job tree. For example we could provide a total solution for hanging doors for our carpenter or the prime contractor. Of course that would limit our scope and potential market opportunities. But it may be a winning and profitable strategy if we can make the job of hanging doors faster, easier and less expensive.

CHAPTER 6

Creating Job Maps To Gain Insights Into Customer Pain Points

WE LEARNED IN Chapter 5 that jobs are made up of discrete process steps with a beginning, middle and end. Whether we are describing a simple job, (for example, receiving a package on the loading dock), or a more complex job that has a hierarchical structure (for example, performing an inventory audit at the end of year), we can deconstruct all jobs from beginning to end. This creates a complete picture of all the steps where customers might struggle and desire more help in getting their jobs done better.

Mapping steps in a job

Mapping out these steps is called "job mapping." Receiving parts and transferring them into inventory is a discrete step in manufacturing products. It's also an example of a job in itself. Having the right amount of inventory available on the manufacturing floor is repeated throughout the job tree and could provide an opportunity to add value for the job executor if it can save him time and money, and make his job easier.

The Plan, Do, Check and Act (PDCA) continuous improvement loop applied to job mapping

Most of us are familiar with Six Sigma and continuous improvement tools that are used to improve quality and overall operational execution. Conceptually, these tools can be applied to help us better understand how customers get their jobs done.

The Plan, Do, Check and Act (PDCA) technique is one of many models we can use as a starting point to break down the process steps involved in executing a job or a chain of jobs.

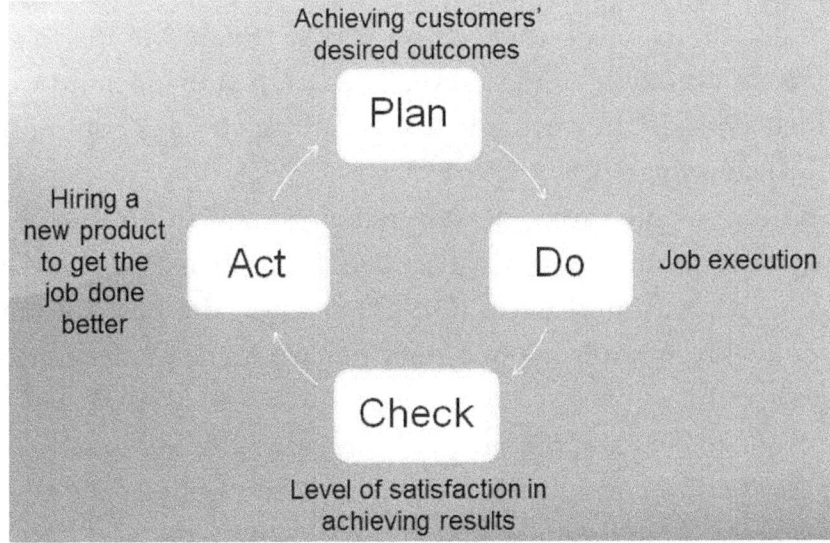

Figure 6.1: *The plan, do, check and act process*

Without realizing it, we apply plan, do, check and act many times each day when trying to get our jobs done, from the very trivial job of getting a morning cup of coffee or juice to start the day off right, to the more complex job of planning a business trip to meet an important client.

People do jobs to achieve desired outcomes

Consciously or unconsciously, we begin a job by planning (plan) what we want to get done (our desired outcome). Then we execute the job (do). After executing the job (or sub-job), we discover what worked and which didn't (check). And we learn (or have an opportunity to learn) what to do differently the next time (act) to achieve better results.

Think in terms of the purpose for the process, not the process itself

The focus of our analysis is not on HOW customers get jobs done currently but rather on WHAT they are trying to get done (desired outcomes) at every step of the job map and why. Which steps do they struggle with? And which steps could possibly be eliminated?

Often people carry out steps in a process without thinking. They don't understand why they are doing them. "It's just the way we do it around here." Or: "That's how the boss told me to do it." It reminds me of a story I heard many years ago that goes like this:

A young girl asked her mother, "Mommy, why do you cut the ends off the meat before you cook it?" The girl's mother replied, "You know, sweetie, I'm not exactly sure. I think it might add to the meat's flavor, but perhaps you should ask your grandmother since she always did it that way."

So the little girl finds her grandmother, climbs up on her lap and asks, "Grandma, why do you and Mommy cut the ends of the meat off before you cook it?" Her grandmother responded, "Well, I don't know about your mom, but I did it because my pot wasn't big enough."

Job maps provide a comprehensive framework to identify the metrics customers use to describe success

Every step on the job map provides us with a clear definition of measurements of success from the customer's perspective. Each step has inputs and outputs associated with it. The degree to which customers struggle with getting the right inputs, and the level of effort needed to execute a step and/or achieve the desired outcomes in executing a step, provide the guidepost for the development team to innovate around.

In Chapter 7 we'll explore desired outcome statements in great depth: what they are, how to uncover them, how to construct them, how to rank them in terms of satisfaction and importance, and finally, which underserved desired outcomes we should focus on to create new value for the customer.

Core concept

Keep an eye on the steps that customers are doing. Are they struggling to get them done? Can we make the steps simpler? Can we eliminate steps completely and simplify their jobs? Can we reduce time and cost? Can we increase their satisfaction and create new value? If we can, the chances are customers will embrace and hire our solutions.

> **Exercise:** Create a job map for an important business activity.
>
> Describe an important job that either your company needs to get done, or perhaps describe an important job your customers want to get done, and create a job map. Keep it high level – we just want to get a feel for what job maps look like.

CHAPTER 7

Defining the customer's success metrics at every step of a job

THE REAL POWER of the jobs-to-be-done innovation approach lies in identifying and prioritizing a set of desired outcomes a customer wants to achieve by executing his job. In Chapters 5 and 6 we discovered that jobs are processes consisting of multiple steps. At each step of a job, a job executor is expecting to achieve specific outcomes.

Customers may not know HOW to get their job steps done better, but they can accurately define their level of satisfaction in getting their current job steps done.

We use qualitative research techniques to probe deeply into the what, why, when of a customer's job, and the circumstances he faces when executing his job. Qualitative research can include site visits, in-depth interviews, ethnographic research or a combination of all of them. In Chapter 12 we'll explore how to conduct exploratory jobs-to-be-done research.

Depending on the complexity of a job, we can expect to uncover from 50 to more than 150[17] desired outcomes during our exploratory research. But the information will come as unstructured data. We have to translate the data into a common structure that we can further test and prioritize in subsequent rounds of quantitative research and concept testing.

How to construct an outcome statement

A desired outcome statement typically states a direction of improvement (to minimize or increase something), a unit of measurement (number, time, frequency, likelihood) and the desired outcome.

For example, if a field technician talks about the steps involved in installing a complex system, we might discover he really struggles with not having the right tool at the job site. Perhaps the right tool was never kitted in his tool box. Or because job sites become visually cluttered and chaotic, tools are misplaced so that the technician has to search for the tool, resulting in frustration and wasted time.

An outcome statement for this example would look like this:

---

17 What Customers Want," Anthony W. Ulwick, The McGraw-Hill Companies, 2005, chapter 2, page 27.

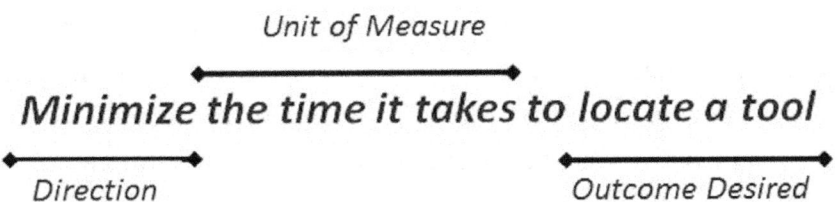

Figure 7.1: *Structure of an outcome statement*

With additional analysis of the unstructured data from the initial research, we might uncover several outcome statements like these:

- Increase the likelihood of finding the right tool
- Increase the likelihood of having the right tool on hand
- Decrease the time it takes to find the right tool
- Decrease the time it takes to store a tool
- Increase the likelihood the tool will not be misplaced
- Increase the likelihood of knowing if a tool is missing before coming to the job site

Structure provides a consistent definition and measurement of job success

It might look as if outcome statements don't provide specific specifications. That is correct. We create specifications and define a specific solution later, during the design and development phases of the new product development cycle.

Collecting hard specifications during the discovery phase of research would mean we had a pre-determined solution in mind. **Remember, a core principle of the jobs-to-be-done innovation framework is that it's not tied to a solution.**

Our objective in the research stage is to get a clear understanding of what the customer is trying to get done, how he defines success in getting job steps done, and where he's struggling to improve his overall satisfaction with his job execution.

We're looking for a sense of general direction of success and associated pains that helps define a trend and the overall desired outcomes the job executor seeks. We don't expect to get hard figures here!

Of course, it can happen that we get some hard specifications during the initial exploration, and that may or may not be good. It may be good if it defines a minimum or maximum parameter of a requirement that must be met. For example, a company might require that all parts received in its warehouse have a specific bar code to streamline their receiving process.

But hard specifications assume requirements based on a current solution. To innovate, we need to look beyond the current solution and imagine novel new ways to help customers achieve better outcomes in getting important jobs done. Perhaps a receiving department could speed up its time from dock to stock by using a Radio Frequency Identification (RFID) tag system and completely eliminate the step of scanning bar codes.

Tip: Be like Columbo[18] - keep an open mind

When conducting jobs-to-be-done innovation research, we're never locked into a solution. We're like Columbo, the TV detective, who keeps an open mind and looks for the nuances and contradictions in the desired outcomes. That's where we can find opportunities to innovate.

In the next chapter, we'll discover how to use outcome statements to create a rich set of unambiguous market-driven data we can innovate around.

---

18 Columbo is an American detective mystery television film series (1968–78, 1989–2003), starring Peter Falk as Columbo, a homicide detective with the Los Angeles Police Department. The show popularized the inverted detective story format. Almost every episode begins by showing the commission of the crime and its perpetrator; the series therefore has no "whodunit" element. The plot revolves mainly around how the perpetrator, whose identity is already known to the audience, will finally be caught and exposed.

CHAPTER 8

Underserved And Overserved Outcomes Provide Guideposts to Innovate Around

RECALL THAT A typical job chain will have anywhere between 50 to more than 150 outcome statements depending on the complexity of the job-to-be-done.

If we were to try to design around every desired outcome from our research, we'd end up with the old problem of creating a product that tries to be all things to all people, but doesn't serve any one job executor segment well.

Instead we need to do more analysis to discover which of the outcomes are important. Of the important outcomes, we'll determine which ones are underserved (i.e. customers are not satisfied with the current outcome), and which are overserved (customers are very satisfied with the outcome. Improving overserved outcomes results in diminishing returns, a form of waste).

Using quantitative research to Analyze outcome statements

Using the simple and unambiguous structure of outcome statements, we can determine the importance and satisfaction level of each outcome for a set of targeted job executors by conducting follow-up quantitative research. For each desired outcome we ask our follow-up survey participants to rate the following:

1. **The importance** of all the jobs, outcomes and constraints using a scale of 1 to 10 where 10 means critically important and 1 means not important at all.
2. **The degree to which they are satisfied** with how the solution they are using today addresses those jobs, outcomes and constraints. Again we use a scale of 1 to 10, where 10 means totally satisfied and 1 means not satisfied at all.

Ranking the outcomes using the "opportunity algorithm[19]"

We determine the priority of outcome statements from the perspective of the customer by using the following formula:

---

19 "What Customers Want," Anthony W. Ulwick, The McGraw-Hill Companies, 2005, chapter 3, page 45.

Opportunity = Importance + Max(Importance − Satisfaction, 0)

To use the formula, we need to determine the percentage of participants giving a rating of 9 or 10 for each importance and corresponding satisfaction.

For example. in the illustration below Outcome 1 has a score of 9.6 for importance. That means that 96 percent of participants ranked the importance of Outcome 1 as a 9 or a 10. And a score of 2.8 for satisfaction means 28 percent of participants rank their level of satisfaction as 9 or 10. Thus for Outcome 1, 9.6 is inserted in the importance variable, and 2.8 is inserted into the satisfaction variable. Plugging it into the formula we get an opportunity index of 16.4.

Ranking Outcomes Using Opportunity Algorithm

Desired Outcomes	Importance	Satisfaction	Opportunity
Outcome 1	9.6	2.8	16.4
Outcome 2	9.0	6.0	12.0
Outcome 3	9.0	3.9	14.1
...	...	...	...
...	...	...	...
Outcome N	8.5	9.3	8.5

Figure 8.1: Ranking outcomes using Opportunity Algorithm

In Figure 8.1 we can immediately see that the greater the importance of an outcome and the lower the satisfaction level for the outcome, the higher the opportunity rating is. Note also for Outcome N, where the satisfaction level is greater than the importance, the formula tells us to insert a 0 for satisfaction (max(importance − satisfaction,0)) resulting in an opportunity rating of 8.5.

A thorough discussion of using the opportunity algorithm is provided in Anthony Ulwick's book *"What Customers Want"* Chapter 3.

The opportunity index provides a focal point for innovation

The **opportunity algorithm** provides a systematic method to rank and prioritize the desired outcomes that will have the highest impact in defining solutions customers will embrace and choose over alternative competing solutions. If an outcome is important and unsatisfied, it's a good indication of an area to explore and exploit for innovation.

On the other hand, outcomes that are unimportant or already satisfied represent little opportunity for improvement and consequently should receive minimum design resources. Making additional improvements in areas that are already overserved is a waste of resources and is likely to add cost without adding additional value.

Determining the innovation sweet spot

When we plot the outcome index scores for each outcome on an X/Y graph, where the X axis represents importance and the Y axis represents satisfaction, we can see how outcomes cluster along specific bands. See Figure 8.2 below.

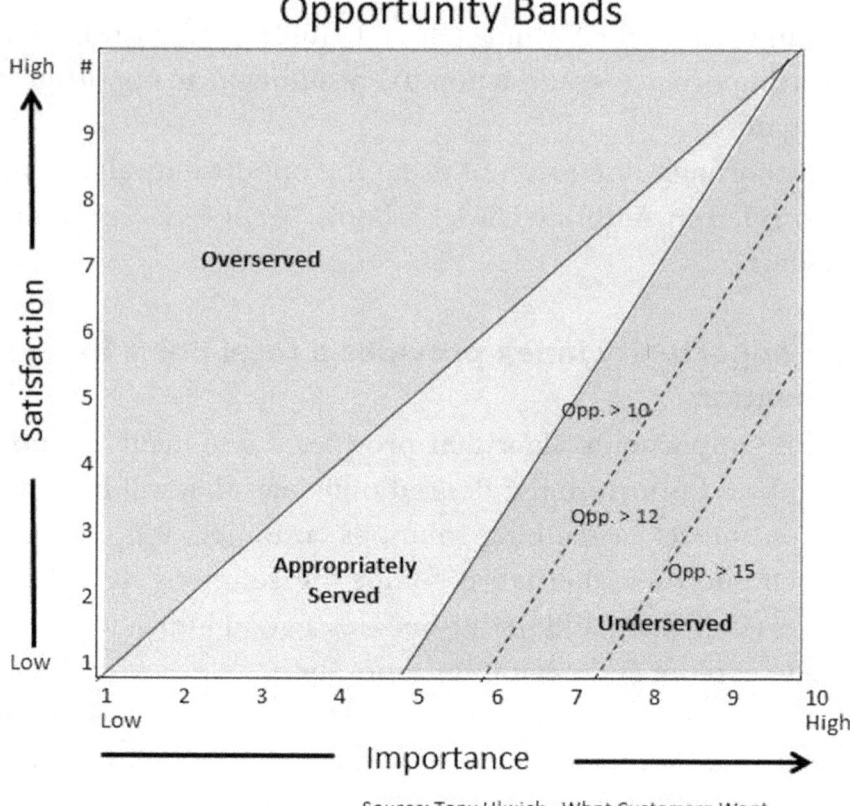

Figure 8.2: Jobs-To-Be-Done opportunity bands

Generally speaking, outcomes with an index score of 15 or greater represent areas of outstanding innovation opportunity. These are opportunities to be explored and exploited as much as possible. Opportunities with indexes of 15 or greater are more often found in new and evolving markets.

Outcomes with scores between 12 and 15 are likely to occur in both established and new markets as products and services rarely execute a job perfectly. They represent the low-hanging fruit the development team should focus its innovation on.

Scores between 10 and 12 are worthy of consideration, though they may not be unique enough to establish a highly differentiated solution. Nevertheless, improvements along these dimensions can yield solutions that separate us from the competitor pack.

Opportunities ranked below 10 are generally considered overserved and won't provide a discriminating competitive advantage no matter how much we invest in improving them. However, because they are overserved, these outcomes might offer an opportunity to reduce overall cost by reducing the performance levels of targeted features, assuming the features remain "good enough."

For example, increasing processor speed for a laptop computer may have very little performance advantage from the user's point of view. But what if we could reduce the speed while extending the battery life of the laptop? Perhaps that would be a better tradeoff to pursue.

Go where the opportunity bands point us

As we gather quantitative data to determine our outcome ranking index, we are also gathering specific information on the customers' current solutions and the corresponding satisfaction levels of each outcome. We can use this competitor data to help shape a differentiated solution and a positioning strategy.

Figure 8.3 is an example of index scores for a small subset of desired outcomes along with the relative satisfaction scores of three competitors. For illustrative purposes, let's say that brand Z represents us, and brand X and Y are the top two competitors in our target area.

Desired Outcome for A tool Organizer	IMP	SAT	Opp	Satisfaction Competitor Brand		
				X	Y	Z
Increase the likelihood of finding the right tool	9.6	2.8	16.4	3.7	2.1	2.7
Decrease the time it takes to find the right tool	9.0	6.0	12.0	7.9	2.3	4.7
Decrease the time it takes to store a tool	9.0	3.9	14.1	6.3	3.2	4.3
Increase the likelihood the tool will not be misplaced	8.5	9.2	8.5	8.0	7.7	7.6
Increase the likelihood of knowing if a tool is missing	4.0	7.0	4.0	8.2	5.4	7.1
Increase the security of storing tools	7.8	4.5	11.1	3.2	5.4	4.2

Figure 8.3: Competitive analysis based on outcomes and satisfaction levels

We can see that **"Increasing the likelihood of finding the right tool"** is an outcome with an index score of 16.4, and a relatively low satisfaction level for all three brands. Thus this would be an outcome we'd want to focus our development resources on to improve it.

If we succeed in creating a solution that moves the customer's satisfaction level toward the ideal product (total satisfaction), we'll achieve a competitive advantage we can enjoy until our competitors follow with their attempt at a competitive response.

"Decreasing the time it takes to find the right tool" also looks like a promising opportunity to focus on. Here though, we see that competitor X has a leg up on the rest of the brands. We could attempt to create a new approach to better competitor's

X solution. Or alternatively, we could simply emulate brand X's solution and achieve competitive parity.

As long as we have sufficient differentiation along other opportunity vectors, this could be a great solution: it reduces our time to market in launching a new product. NOTE: We certainly don't want to emulate competitor Y's solution since they have the worst score amongst the three solutions. Emulating their design solution will set us back in the minds of the customers.

Finally the opportunity **"Increase the likelihood of knowing if a tool is missing"** receives a 4 on the opportunity index. This suggests that the opportunity is overserved and not worth focusing development efforts on. Let competitor X continue to spend development resources on improving this outcome vector: money spent on an overserved outcome is wasted effort.

Final thoughts

Using the jobs-to-be-done innovation method, we can discover what customers are really trying to achieve by doing specific jobs, how they measure success, and the circumstances, challenges and obstacles that get in their way of achieving 100 percent satisfaction in executing the job.

We now know that important jobs-to-be-done will typically have from 50 to more than 150 desired outcomes in their job chains. By using the opportunity algorithm we can determine the best opportunities by identifying the most important outcomes with the least satisfaction (underserved outcomes) while identifying the marginal opportunities (unimportant outcomes and/or outcomes already satisfied).

With this information, we can direct our development efforts towards creating a highly differentiated and desirable solution that customers want. Or even better, create a whole new market segment – a Blue Ocean[20] – where we create new rules of the game to attract and retain new customers who are left out of the existing market.

In the next chapter we'll discover how the jobs-to-be-done innovation approach provides us with a lens into defining new markets and product categories that result in breakthrough innovation.

---

20 Blue Ocean Strategy – W. Chan Kim and Renée Mauborgne. Based on a study of 150 strategic moves spanning more than a hundred years and thirty industries, Kim & Mauborgne show that companies can succeed not by battling competitors, but rather by creating "blue oceans" of uncontested market space. These strategic moves create a leap in value for the company, its buyers, and its employees, while unlocking new demand and making the competition irrelevant. The book presents analytical frameworks and tools that foster an organization's ability to systematically create and capture blue oceans.

CHAPTER 9

To Innovate Take Off Your Product-Oriented Blinders

IT'S QUITE NATURAL to be product oriented, especially if we've been in a market that was clamoring for our products. All we have to do is to improve our products incrementally, stay slightly ahead of our competition with better product specs and performance, and trust that our sales force would keep selling like mad.

That's what it looks like when we're in a growth market. But unfortunately that changes in a more competitive market environment. Customers eventually find better solutions to address their jobs-to-be-done. That's when we're likely to miss out on the next wave of innovation, because we're stuck in our old success models and we lose touch with the fundamental jobs customers are trying to get done.

Ford once upon a time really was number one

It reminds me of the story of Henry Ford and his Model T car. In 1908 when Ford introduced the Model T (also known as the Tin Lizzie), it was by all definitions a huge success and a game changer, not only for the auto industry but for the overall transportation industry at the time. It was so revolutionary that, in an international poll, it was named the most influential car in the world in the 20th century.[21]

The Model T was the iPad of its time. People had seen nothing quite like it before. Sure there were lots of automakers around, but nobody put the pieces together in the way that old Henry did – literally! (The assembly line was one of Ford's major innovations).

But by the 1920s the auto industry had matured. Consumer tastes had changed and consumers were looking for greater variety in driving experiences than what the Tin Lizzie offered. Ford stubbornly believed the Model T was all people really needed, and in any color as long as it was black. Ford's refusal to adapt to the times and consumer tastes almost destroyed his company.

If not for his son Edsel's persistence in adapting to the new realities of the market, the Ford Company may not have survived the 1920s because Henry was stuck seeing the world through his product-oriented eyes.

Using a reverse jobs-to-be-done marketing lens to change from a product to a jobs orientation

It's not that difficult to shift from a product to a jobs orientation. The key is to realize that people hire (or buy) products to get important jobs done. All we need to do to reorient our

---

21 The Model T Ford was named most influential car in the world in the 20th century http://en.wikipedia.org/wiki/Ford_Model_T

view is to figure out what those jobs are and how satisfied customers are in getting those jobs done.

The questions we need answers to are:

1. What jobs are people trying to get done by hiring our products?
2. What are the ultimate outcomes they want by doing these jobs?
3. Is this the primary job or is it one step in a chain of jobs?
4. What circumstances and constraints do they face in executing their jobs?
5. From their perspective, how satisfied are they with the outcomes they are currently achieving in getting their jobs done?

An example of using a reverse jobs-to-be-done marketing lens to spot new opportunities

Let's take an office product and look at it through a reverse jobs-to-be-done marketing lens. Let's use the scanner sitting on the corner of my very cluttered desk.

Why do customers hire scanners?

Well, of course, to digitize documents and images. But why? What are they really trying to get done by digitizing documents? Perhaps they want to organize their work flow better and get rid of all the clutter in their office. Or it could be that they want to share documents or pictures with others.

But maybe what they really want is to improve their overall productivity by simplifying how they manage, store, access and control information. Scanning paper documents is only one of many jobs in the job chain of managing information within their workflow. Perhaps they really struggle in locating stored documents and are concerned about how safe and secure the documents will be in storage, digital or otherwise.

Document management is a well-established job category at the enterprise level. But document solution providers can benefit by looking at the total job flow involved in transforming information into knowledge and enterprise wisdom, as seen from the user's perspective.

And besides large enterprises, who else has similar jobs to be done? What about small and home offices? Are these job executors managing paper and information flow in their work environments in a way that helps them achieve the outcomes they desire? Would they adopt new products and ideas if a scanner maker opened its lens to really see how people are dealing with paper and information overload, and then came up with a simple cost effective solution? I think so.

> **Exercise:** Why do people hire your products and services?
>
> Apply the reverse jobs-to-be-done marketing lens on one of your products or services and explore the core jobs people are trying to get done by hiring your solutions.
>
> Start by answering these questions about your products and services:
>
> 1. What jobs are people trying to get done by hiring our products?
>
> 2. What are the ultimate outcomes they want by doing these jobs?

3. Is this the primary job or is it one step in a chain of jobs?

4. What circumstances and constraints do they face in executing their jobs?

5. From their perspective, how satisfied are they with the outcomes they are currently achieving in getting their jobs done?

CHAPTER 10

A Great Idea? Or A Solution Looking For A Problem?

A POTENTIAL INVENTION can look great on paper and in the R&D lab, but if it doesn't fundamentally address a specific outcome customers want to accomplish, or overcome a specific constraint that's standing in their way, then chances are the product concept will fail in the market.

A lot of my tech clients do a fantastic job of coming up with technology based ideas that could be the "next big thing." Where they get stuck though is defining a value proposition and business model that has market appeal. The reason they get stuck is that they don't have a good innovation framework to validate the concept and define real user requirements that customers will value and want.

So instead, they march forward in the development process only to discover that they have created a product that is a solution looking for a problem to solve. And/or a product that potential customers simple don't understand (muddled value proposition). The product doesn't quite fit anyone's pain and they are having a difficult time describing what the product does and for which customers.

Defining value from the customer's perspective

Before marching down the development process, we can use the jobs-to-be-done marketing lens in reverse order to identify potential and real jobs that people are trying to get done where our technology can be applied to get their jobs done better, faster and cheaper.

Starting with the technology and it's benefits and unique attributes, start asking the following questions to form a preliminary customer value proposition that you can test, verify and refine.

- What are the capabilities of the solution/technology?
- What barriers does it overcome?
- What objectives/desired outcomes can it address?
- In what circumstance will it be most effective?
- What constraints does it overcome?
- What jobs does the solution apply to?
- Who would hire this solution for this job?

We should be able to come up with several potential jobs-to-be-done and circumstances where your solution has potential appeal. The next step in the innovation process is to tighten up the potential range of target customers by doing some quick and dirty market research, mostly secondary research to see what's out there and what products and services customers' are currently hiring to get their jobs done, while getting a general sense of the scope of the business opportunity.

If we aren't finding a lot of information on what jobs people are trying to get done and their current "how they get it done," you may very well find that either our technology doesn't match a real problem or the technology is still too early in the adoption cycle to be commercially viable at this time.

If the concept is a promising new technology in the early stages of market adoption, most likely you will find a lot of secondary data to suggest that there is a lot of interest, at least from potential future competitors and industry evangelist. This should provide enough evidence to continue to explore and develop the concept.

At this stage of the process, we should have a preliminary business hypothesis and customer value proposition that can be tested to validate, refine and/or steer us to a more compelling problem your technology and solution set solves.

An example of using the reverse jobs-to-be-done marketing lens

Let's explore an example of how a technology team can transform an interesting idea into a commercial success. The product idea we're going to explore is fictitious but is based on a composite of several real concepts and products that both my clients and I have successfully brought to market using this process.

We'll assume our development team has come up with a wireless sensor technology that appears to have a set of attributes that make it unique and that offers better potential than other technologies currently on the market. But the team also knows it lacks certain performance attributes and, in certain situations, this makes their technology inferior to other product offerings.

The wireless sensor technology provides superior low power performance that extends battery life significantly, is potentially superior in cost performance (component cost is less), but lacks data capacity and signal range (low data rates and short range – better than passive RFID tags but not as good as a 802.15.4 radio used on ZigBee[22] products and the like).

The development team was confident it has the expertise and capability to build the product, but they hadn't yet found a market or business model that makes enough sense to justify moving forward. The product was in their white space (it's new to them and new to the market) but they believe it has huge possibilities if they can identify a job-to-be-done that isn't getting done well.

At this stage of the process the development team begins hypothesizing possible uses for the technology by using the reverse jobs-to-be-done marketing lens. They define potential and actual jobs that people are trying to get done, where this new solution becomes an obvious choice for them to hire.

They begin their exploration by asking the following questions to form a preliminary customer value proposition that they will test, verify and refine.

- What are the capabilities of the solution/technology?
    - Wireless network technology that can monitor low data rate sensors, assets and other things.

---

22 ZigBee is a wireless technology developed as an open global standard to address the unique needs of low-cost, low-power wireless machine-to-machine networks.

- - Extremely low power so it can operate a long time before needing a new battery.
  - Extremely small so it's easy to embed into devices.

- What barriers does it overcome?
  - Makes monitoring a wide variety of functions extremely simple and cost effective.
  - Because it's small and can last a long time on one battery, it can be embedded into devices and run for a prolong period of time. This eliminates the hassle and expense of having to replace batteries, a task that for some embedded applications is nearly impossible.

- What objectives/desired outcomes can it address?
  - Automating the monitoring of critical equipment and machinery over an extended period of time – years not months!
  - Keeping tabs on the location of assets, especially assets on the move. Better than RFID tags because it doesn't require super close proximity.

- In what circumstance will it be most effective?
  - Low data rates so it's good for sensors and item tracking.
  - In applications that need to run a long time without having to send people into the field to replace batteries, especially where there are lots of these sensors out there and where they're hard to get to.

- What constraints does it overcome?
  - A simple way to monitor things – be it simple sensor data or tracking assets – without having to invest people resources to do the task.

- For what jobs is the solution applicable?
  - We looked at a lot of potential applications. We believe if we could embed our wireless sensors into hand tools, we can help job site workers be more productive: we can help them keep tabs on their tools, from making sure they have the right set of tools in their tool box before heading to the site, to helping them find tools they put down for a moment but don't remember where, and perhaps also helping them maintain their tools by providing maintenance and calibration warnings.

- Who would hire this solution for this job?
  - There are many job executors we think can benefit from using our location aware tools, from commercial construction job workers to the weekend home repair person.
  - We think, though, that commercial construction and equipment installation and repair users offer the best opportunity because of the size and scope of what we believe is a big pain to solve.

Now we can formulate a basic job-to-be-done hypothesis:
"construction and field workers are constantly losing their tools or forgetting to bring the right tools and parts onto the job site. If there

was a simple way for them to kit up their tool box before coming to the site as well as a way to help them find a tool that they put down somewhere only to lose sight of it and search for ever to find – they'd be more productive and less frustrated in getting their construction jobs done."

We'll assume the team does some preliminary secondary research and finds evidence that there is potential for a product like this. However the evidence is still fuzzy and they aren't ready to take a giant leap of faith. Refer to chapter 8 were we discuss how to use jobs-to-be-done market research to test, validate and refine preliminary business hypotheses.

> **Exercise:** Apply the reverse jobs-to-be-done lens on a promising technology.
>
> Let's say your development team has created a very novel approach to creating a satellite antenna that is far thinner and lighter than anything on the market today. It's so thin that it could easily be mounted inside the roof of a car to provide internet communication on the go.
>
> But it also has limited gain and may not work with conventional earth orbiting communication satellite systems depending on the latitude (north and south location) where the antenna is located.
>
> Given the capabilities and constraints of your antenna system, identify potential jobs-to-be-done and circumstances where the antenna has potential appeal.

CHAPTER 11

Market Segmentation Using The Jobs-To-Be-Done Marketing Lens

DETERMINING HOW TO segment the market is one of the most critical decisions a company makes in planning its overall strategy to achieve its growth goals. The goal of market segmentation is to divide customers into groups that share unmet needs that are different from customers in other groups. These groups of customers with similar unmet needs represent unique segments of opportunity.

Market segmentation is both an analytical and a creative process. It involves collecting and analyzing data about the potential market. Then our marketing and innovation teams interpret the data imaginatively. It takes hard work, reflection and a willingness to explore outside the current or obvious segments. This is especially true for early market opportunities.

Done right though, segmentation provides the foundation and game plan for developing products and services that are aligned with the demands and wants of our targeted segments. In addition, it determines the positioning strategy and direction for our ongoing marketing and sales activities.

It seems that market segmentation would be an integral component of product strategy and planning, that companies would invest the time and resources to really understand potential market segments. After all, when we define our segments and organize them into unique groups of user needs, we can target them with new product platforms or disruptive and sustainable innovations. Our probability of commercial success improves dramatically.

Overreliance on demographic or geographic segmentation schemas

Then why do so many marketers and innovation teams still apply superficial market segmentation strategies? There are a couple of reasons:

1) They've always done it that way. And that's the way most marketing books tell us how to do it.

2) It's easy to get product data, geographic data and often demographic data, since this data is typically included as part of the transactional records.

3) Thinking about market segmentation strategically is hard work! While simple to understand, it can be hard to carry out.

Demographic and geographic information might help us locate customers so we can formulate a communication strategy. But even if we know that a person belongs to a certain age group and ethnicity, that doesn't tell us much about that person's unique situation, pain, wants, values or the problems they want solved.

Daniel Yankelovich in his classic HBR article *"New Criteria For Market Segmentation23"* had this to say about using demographic data for segmenting markets:

"[.......] finding marketing opportunities by depending solely on demographic breakdowns is like trying to win a national election by relying only on the information in a census. A modern census contains useful data, but it identifies neither the crucial issues of an election, nor those groups whose voting habits are still fluid, nor the needs, values, and attitudes that influence how those groups will vote. This kind of information, rather than census-type data, is the kind that wins elections—and markets."

What segmentation schemas should we use to segment the market?

There are several ways to cut and aggregate markets into segments. There is no one right way and it will probably take several iterations before we come to a clear and useful definition of the market.

Again referring back to Yankelovich:

"The point at issue is not that demographic segmentation should be disregarded, but rather that it should be regarded as only one among many possible ways of analyzing markets. In fact, the key requirement of segmentation analysis is that the marketing director should never assume in advance that any one method of segmentation is the best.

---

23 "New Criteria For Market Segmentation." Daniel Yankelovich, HBR March/April 1964

His first job should be to muster all probable segmentation and then choose the most meaningful ones to work with."

Common market segmentation schemas

- Demographic segmentation is based on variables such as age, gender, family size, income, occupation, education, religion, race and nationality.
- Behavior segmentation is based on variables such as usage rate and patterns, price sensitivity and brand loyalty.
- Psychographic segmentation is based on variables such as values, attitudes and lifestyle.
- Product type/category segmentation is based on product attributes such as entry level, premium products, price points and functional set.

For business markets, we often apply additional schemas:

- Geographic segmentation is based on regional variables such as customer concentration, regional industrial growth rate and international macroeconomic factors.
- Customer type is based on factors such as the size of the organization, its industry and its position in the value chain.
- Buyer behavior is based on factors such as loyalty to suppliers, usage patterns and order size.

These schemas give us information, but not the information we really need to innovate. Specifically, they don't tell us what products and services people really want and are willing to pay for to get rid of a pain.

Viewing segmentation from the customer's perspective

When we look at the full spectrum of people trying to get specific jobs done, we discover that **different people have different struggles when executing their jobs-to-be-done**. Using **opportunity scores** (discussed in Chapter 8) to analyze outcomes and constraints, we uncover natural segments within the data set by clustering opportunity scores into logical subsets.

Using opportunity scores to find clusters of underserved outcomes is a more relevant market segmentation schema for the innovator. These logical subsets define viable market opportunities that we can base our innovation and new product development activities around. When we address these important outcomes, we'll have a high likelihood of market success.

Once we identify a job segment or segments, and we understand customer characteristics within that job segment, we can apply other segment schemas to complete the profile. With this information, our new product development and marketing teams can develop a winning marketing strategy to capture the customer's loyalty.

Final words from Yankelovich on market segmentation strategy:

"Markets should be scrutinized for important differences in buyer attitudes, motivations, values, usage patterns, aesthetic preferences, or degree of susceptibility. These may have no demographic correlatives. Above all, we must never assume in advance that we know the best way of looking at a market."

We need to know what important jobs people are trying to get done, and how different groups have different struggles carrying out the target jobs. Then we can tailor products and marketing strategies that address the unique needs of that targeted job segment: our odds of launching a new product successfully are almost guaranteed.

> **Exercise:** Come up with a segmentation strategy using jobs-to-be-done marketing lens.
>
> Take a look at your current customers and the important jobs they are trying to get done. Come up with a segmentation strategy based on their desired outcomes and struggles. Or perhaps examine the market segmentation strategy of a familiar company to you: Perhaps Zipcars or Tesla, or Segway as an example of poor segmentation strategy.

CHAPTER 12

The ABC's of Conducting Jobs-To-Be-Done Market Research

UP TO THIS point, most of our jobs investigation is based on high level inputs from both internal and external experts and from end users. The initial ideas and concepts we generate are transformed into preliminary job statements by asking a series of questions [see chapter 9 *section "Using a "reverse" jobs-to-be-done marketing lens to change from a product to jobs oriented perspective"]* that uncover the essence of the types of jobs customers are potentially trying to get done using our untested value proposition.

In Chapter 5 we learned that before we can conduct formal research, we need to formulate a preliminary job statement or statements to investigate. There may be more than one, but there shouldn't be more than 3 or 4, otherwise our research will be too random to validate if the job(s) we're investigating is (are) important and underserved.

Using qualitative and quantitative research techniques to uncover desired outcomes

The first phase of the formal research is primarily qualitative. Our objective is to discover which important jobs our research subjects are trying to get done, why they're doing those jobs in the first place, and their overall level of satisfaction in executing and achieving their desired outcomes.

Our research needs to have a structure that keeps the conversation focused on the specific job statement under investigation. At the same time, it should allow enough flexibility to probe deeper into what customers are trying to get done and why, and what's working and not working for them. We want our subjects to tell us their story as they see it, not as we want them to see it.

Adding structure to our research

We create structure by formulating specific quantitative questions based on a modified Likert scale with a numerical range of 1-10 with descriptive anchors at each end. The quantitative questions help guide the conversation so we understand the jobs customers are trying to get done and their level of satisfaction in getting those jobs done.

Suppose we wanted to investigate if construction workers really need a solution to make sure they bring the right tools to a job site, and to help prevent them from losing tools on the site, so they can get their project jobs done better. (See **Constructing a job statement in** Chapter 5).

The quantitative questions act as anchor text to keep the conversation focused on job under investigation, desired outcomes and the circumstance a job executor faces when trying to get an important job done.

Anchor questions also help us search and analyze the data set after all the interviews are completed. This is especially helpful if we are searching twenty or more interview transcripts since it's very difficult and time-consuming to search an unstructured data set.

A good anchor question to use:

"On a scale of 1 to 10 where 1 = not satisfied, 5 = somewhat, and 10 = totally satisfied, where would you rank your satisfaction with having the right tools on the construction site to get your work done?"

Not satisfied 1 2 3 4 5 6 7 8 9 10 Totally satisfied

The key to the initial phase of the jobs-to-be-done research is that the real value of the numerical rating lies not in the number itself but in the explanation of why the number was chosen. We can combine the rating scale with a follow-up question asking: "What would it take to make it a 10?" Or: "Why did you give it a ranking of 6?

The follow-on discussions yield in-depth information about the specific components of the score, what elements the respondent used to judge the item in the question, the missing "wow's" and the existing pains and impediments.

High and low scores provide trend information

Additional analysis of the combined scores of all respondents helps us to understand the range of answers, high and low scores, and trends. We need to use our judgment in analyzing the data to define what is a high score and what is a low score, especially for small data sets.

In looking at how scores cluster, we might decide that scores between 8 and 10 can be counted as high and scores of 6 and below are considered low.

The real value of the numbers is to act as focal points for analyzing the verbatim transcripts of the interviews. We can then compare opinions (and quotes) associated with high scores to those associated with low scores. We can identify definite themes and use them to gain valuable insights.

Quantifying job and outcome importance and satisfaction levels

In conducting the jobs-to-be-done research phase, we collect a tremendous amount of data on the important jobs customers want to get done, and on how satisfied they are in achieving their desired outcomes. If we followed the structured interview plan described in the previous section, we'll have a rich set of data we can use to gain immediate insights into the customer's circumstances and needs.

But we can mine many more insights from the interview data than just from the raw transcripts. In this section, I'll walk you through how to take raw transcript data and restructure it into desired outcome statements that we'll use to conduct the quantitative portion of our research.

Transforming raw unstructured data into quantifiable data

Let's take a look of some actual transcripts from a research project I did for a client. In this particular jobs-to-be-done research, my client had a promising new technology that could make the job of deploying wireless sensor networks (WSN) easier (the initial job-to-be-done under investigation.)

However, at the time of the investigation, wireless sensor networks were not yet widely deployed. There was no clear ready-made market needing wireless sensors that my client could exploit.

Using the reverse jobs-to-be-done marketing lens, (see chapter 10 for an example of how to use the reverse jobs-to-be-done marketing lens) we explored what important jobs customers are doing today, that they could potentially improve by using wireless sensor networks. We came up with several potential jobs and created a hypothesis for a very important job wireless sensor networks could improve:

"Monitoring industrial equipment remotely to make sure important equipment is operating at its maximum efficiency."

Our research pointed us to an industry based on **Condition Based Maintenance (CBM)**. CBM companies provide solutions to help their customers maintain and improve equipment efficiencies. We had reason to believe this was a good market for us to explore.

Now the question was: "How could wireless sensors and my client's technology get the job of condition based monitoring done better?" That was the core jobs-to-be-done hypothesis we would investigate.

Structuring an outcome statement

In Chapter 7 we learned that an outcome statement has the following structure:

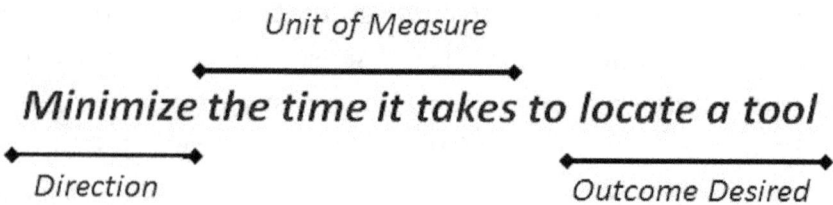

Figure 12.1: Structure of an Outcome Statement

With the outcome statement structure in mind, let's see what kind of outcome statements we can create from actual data:

Outcome statement example 1:

"There's certain equipment in our plant that's hard to get to, or impossible to get to when it's running."

Outcome statements from this snippet might be:

- Increase the likelihood of monitoring hard to reach equipment in an industrial plant
- Increase the likelihood of monitoring equipment (with moving parts) while running

Outcome statement example 2:

"End users [maintenance professional] value [condition based monitoring] but higher up the chain they don't – for them [condition based monitoring] must be connected to business value"

- Increase the likelihood upper management will understand the value and ROI of condition based monitoring systems

- Minimize the cost of deploying and operating condition based monitoring solutions

These are simple examples of creating outcome statements by analyzing interview transcripts. There'll be an enormous amount of data and information to extract from the interviews. Basic patterns in the responses will emerge that we can cluster and combine, making it easier to identify and extract outcome statements.

If you'd like a summary of our actual wireless sensor networks jobs-to-be-done research, you can find it on our website: http://inpdcenter.com/resources/wireless-sensor-adoption-study-key-findings/. The study provides more information on how we did the research, the questions we asked, who we asked and the preliminary results.

CHAPTER 13

Tips On Managing And Conducting Customer Interviews

Manage your interview time

FOR A 60-MINUTE interview, you should have 10 to 15 anchor questions to facilitate the conversation. It's not unusual to dive deeply into one or two questions. Valuable information comes when you probe deeper into a subject's story allowing him or her to share experiences of getting jobs done. Manage your time as best you can and make sure you get to the core questions that focus on job importance and satisfaction level.

Don't worry if you can't get all your questions answered. Trust me, you'll get a lot of important and relevant information in a 60-minute interview if you keep to your research structure. Be respectful of your subject's time. If you say the interview will be 60 minutes, then make sure it's no more than 60 minutes.

A note about interview transcripts

Whenever possible, you should record your interviews and have them transcribed for post interview analysis. And of course, you should always ask permission in advance to record your subjects.

If you explain to them why you are recording the interviews, and how their information will be used, especially regarding confidentiality, most subjects will say yes. Here's an example of a script I've used successfully to get permission to record jobs-to-be-done interviews:

"(Subjects name), all answers to this survey will be held in the strictest of confidence. Respondents identification will not be linked to any information without prior approval by the respondent."

This establishes confidentiality and the protocol on requiring permission to quote subjects in subsequent research reports. Then I might say:

"With your permission, of course, I'd like to tape the interview so that I can be sure I record your comments accurately and don't lose any important information due to my scribbling. Would that be all right?"

Sometimes subjects don't want to be recorded. You can still capture excellent information by taking detailed notes. This is why it's a good idea to have at least one other person on the interviewing team in charge of taking notes.

If you record the interviews, transcribe the audio files into Word files. There are many good transcription services that provide great value. Most, if not all, of the data mining will come from the transcripts, though you might want to listen to selected parts of the audio files to uncover nuances that might provide additional insights. If you don't have audio, you'll have to rely on your notes.

Use Excel to organize your data. Each anchor question (quantitative questions, demographic questions and the scripted qualitative questions) is listed on an Excel sheet. Each sheet will include all respondents' inputs including their Likert scores and follow-on qualitative responses to the drill down questions.

You'll have to decide how many quotes (and their lengths) you want to include for each question. There'll be a lot of information to sort through and it can be overwhelming as you get into the analysis. I recommend capturing all the quotes that offer insights and pasting them into the appropriate Excel sheet. You'll do several recursions of data mining and report formatting to identify unique and insightful information that contains specific desired outcomes.

In your notes, try to capture key phrases so you can do a simple text search to locate the quote in the text. If you mark the time you can also search the audio file. You'll discover amazing nuggets so do a little upfront planning to help guide your mining efforts to the right spots.

It's relatively straightforward to create the quantitative charts and statistics in Excel. The challenge is to decide how to "quantize" the data (i.e. what range of numbers represents high ratings and what range of numbers represents low ratings). This can be especially tricky if the data set is relatively small (less than 25). Don't sweat it though. All you're doing is looking for trends to develop a general idea of what potential customers want and value.

In this early stage research you'll get some level of validation as to whether the jobs-to-be-done are important or not important. You'll also gain new insights and opportunities you may not have otherwise been aware of. This is the power of the discovery driven design process – and it's a process. You still have more work to do in mining the data and in all likelihood uncovering more questions to test.

The research team

I recommend having a minimum of two people on your interview team but no more than three.

- Lead interviewer. This is the most important person, someone who is trained in probing and listening skills. Ideally this person isn't emotionally attached to the project so as not to introduce confirmation bias (asking questions and then hearing answers that unfairly confirm and/or refute the hypotheses under test).

  Consider hiring a professional interviewer who is trained in the techniques of **Voice of Customer (VoC)** interviewing and who won't have a personal stake in the results (i.e. not biased one way or the other). Yes, this can be an internal person but if it's a project lead, be careful that cognitive bias is not introduced.

- Observer, scribe and domain expert. The role of this person is primarily to listen and observe the interview conversation. Having two sets of ears provides a more diverse interpretation of the rich data set you'll create. This person can also clarify questions as well as help drill deeper on key response threads.
- You have to be cautious though. The domain expert must not go into selling mode or influence the test

subject in any manner. He or she must follow the lead interviewer and not dominate the conversation.
- Third observer and second scribe. One more set of ears never hurts. If possible rotate team members to sit in on the visit or call. Hearing inputs first-hand builds additional user empathy. Again this person needs to be an observer and not participate in the discussion unless prompted to do so by the lead interviewer.

This is a judgment call but generally speaking I recommend sticking to the allotted time. If you're running over time, ask the subject if they're willing to spend a couple more minutes with you to wrap up the conversation. Remember subjects are doing you a huge favor so respect their time and don't abuse the privilege.

What if we don't cover all the questions?

Depending on the amount and depth of your questions, there's a very good chance you'll run out of time. You'll find the voice of customer conversations to be extremely engaging and time will fly by. Two recommendations for you:

1. Prioritize the key questions that you must have answered and accept the fact that not all of the questions you want to explore will get addressed.

2. Stick to your interview script and manage your time. Move the conversation along. Some of your subjects will want to talk and talk. You'll need to actively facilitate the conversation to keep on track.

Wrapping up the interview

As you're wrapping things up, and assuming you've have created a good rapport with the interviewee, by all means ask for referrals to other people who they believe can provide you good insights. I've found this to be a great way to find qualified people to talk to while also getting a warm lead.

Before you end the conversation, ask the subject **if it's okay to contact them again to clarify any answers they provided.** Most people will agree. Many of the subjects will evolve into future sources of information. They may develop other deeper relationships with you as the concept evolves from idea to great product.

I've touched on only a few of the techniques in conducting the interviews. This should give you a good start. Again if you plan to do a formal voice of customer project it pays to get a trained voice of customer lead to help define and execute the project. It's worth the investment.

CHAPTER 14

Identifying Research Subjects

Finding the right job executors and stakeholders for our research

FOR OUR EARLY voice of customer research (evaluating the preliminary customer value proposition and business model) we're most interested in finding test subjects who are representative of the actual job executors. We also want to identify relevant stakeholders along the consumption chain (decision makers, influencers and possible channel members - anyone who is involved in executing the job-to-be-done.)

If our target market is construction workers at job sites, we'd look for a sample set of construction workers, supervisors, crib tool managers, buyers and their managers to interview. We might also want to find people involved with selling equipment to the target market. They can give us insights into the buying process.

Finding job executors who are willing to spend time providing inputs to us can be challenging, especially if we don't have a prior relationship with them. This is often the case when dealing with early market products and innovations that are outside our current business model. We can't shortcut this process and take the path of least resistance by talking to people who aren't involved with executing the job-to-be-done. That won't give us any relevant insights to work from.

Unless we have lots of resources (people, time and thick skin), I don't recommend cold calling prospective subjects. Cold calling is never fun and there's a good chance we'll meet with a lot of resistance and rejection. Even the best sales people don't like cold calling: there's a high probability of getting a lot of hang ups and no one likes that.

It's better to network by using referrals and other warm calling techniques. Perhaps our target market is pretty close to our existing market, for example we're researching a concept that represents a new job-to-be-done for existing customers. If that's the case we can enlist both our sales channels and personal relationships with customers to find the right interview prospects.

When we have no market presence, we'll need to rely on networking techniques. We start with some of the preliminary people we contacted in the early stages of formulating our initial product and business hypotheses. People quoted in secondary research can also be good subjects and/or good referrals.

We can identify people in our networks who know the people we're trying to locate. LinkedIn is one good resource for this.

Test subjects who completed the interview are another great source of referrals. If we did a good job of building rapport throughout the interview, most test subjects are willing to provide the names of a couple of other people they know who can help with our research. It's best to ask them at the end of the interview though, never at the beginning.

Qualifying your research subjects

In the initial contact with a research subject we want to both qualify them and make it easy for them to say yes to the interview. We'll need to offer them something in return for their time. Providing research results to potential subjects (edited to protect your intellectual property) is often a great incentive. Or we can offer other reports or incentives that your subjects would find of value and interest. Though we could offer to pay them for their time, many may not find that idea appealing.

The goal of the first contact is to find out if they are both qualified and interested in helping. They may be neither. If that happens we'll need to do more networking. We don't want to waste their time or ours interviewing someone who doesn't add insight to our research. As in sales, a no is better than no response at all.

If we have the resources (time and money) and the subject is open, we want to arrange a face-to-face interview. Although that's sometimes hard to achieve, face-to-face interviews provide an extra level of insights. Phone interviews work perfectly well too, so face-to-face is a bonus, not a requirement to be successful.

Customer visit matrix

Before we start networking and warm calling, we create a customer visit matrix listing who we plan to call, for what purpose (interviewee and/or referral) and their basic demographics (job executor, expert, supervisor, buyer, channel member, etc.). Then we develop a good script so we communicate clearly and precisely. We keep it crisp and to the point, so we get them engaged.

We may need several calls and emails to connect with people in our targeted network. Some of them we'll never reach. That's part of the process, not a reason to become discouraged. We keep a log of our contact activity till we reach our targeted goal of test subjects. That may be as few as 15 but no more than 50 for the early stage of our voice of customer project.

We continue networking till we find the right mix of people to have insightful conversations with. Not everyone will want to participate. That's why it's essential to get organized so we can network our way to success.

What's next in our jobs-to-be-done investigation?

At this stage, we have mined a tremendous amount of insights and information we can use to start the product definition phase. Our success rate will improve greatly once we understand the important jobs customers want done, the desired outcomes they want to achieve and how they measure success in executing their jobs.

However, we need to keep in mind that we have not yet ranked the information in this phase by importance and satisfaction. In **Chapter 8: Underserved And Overserved Outcomes Provide Guideposts To Innovate Around**, we explored how we use quantitative research to identify important underserved and overserved outcomes we can innovate around to create highly differentiated products that the market has validated for us.

The jobs-to-be-done innovation framework is a repeatable process that takes a lot of the guesswork out of defining a winning new product strategy. But it's not only useful for defining a winning set of product and/or service requirements: it also gives us insight in creating an overall marketing and sales playbook to attract and retain new customers.

> **Exercise:** Validating and honing Teknovantage's core business hypothesis.
>
> A fictitious company we'll call Teknovantage, has identified a promising business opportunity based on what they believe is an important job-to-be-done:
>
> **Construction workers want to have the right tools, equipment and materials within in easy reach and not have to go searching for them when working in messy and cluttered work sites.**
>
> The Teknovantage senior management team isn't sure if they truly have a great opportunity to exploit or if they're caught in the proverbial solution–looking-for-a-problem conundrum. They've asked us to conduct additional research to validate and refine the core job-to-be-done concept.
>
> We want to create a preliminary jobs-to-be-done research project to confirm, refine or refute the initial jobs concept. We need to come up with a research plan that includes:
>
> - Three to four research anchor questions and a follow-on script that drills deeper into each anchor question.

- A preliminary customer visit matrix listing who we plan to call (job executor, expert, supervisor, buyer, channel member, etc.), and for what purpose (interviewee and/or referral).

- An initial contact script that communicates the purpose of contacting subjects on our visit matrix and letting them know what's in it for them.

CHAPTER 15

The Innovator's Playbook For Predictable and Sustainable Growth

THE JOBS-TO-BE-DONE INNOVATION framework provides the structure and a repeatable process to dive deeply into a customer's problem set. It helps us understand the important jobs people need to get done, their specific desired outcomes and what gets in their way of achieving 100 percent satisfaction.

The salient point of the framework is that **it's all about customers achieving their desired outcomes**. Jobs are the activities they do to achieve those outcomes We can think of jobs and outcomes as different sides of the same coin. Any step in the job map, where a job executor struggles to get jobs done, offers an opportunity to discover a winning product concept.

In this chapter, we'll look at how to use the jobs-to-be-done innovation framework as the foundation for creating an innovation playbook to achieve the desired business outcome: **market success!**

What is the innovator's playbook?

The innovator's playbook is the guide and roadmap a company uses to discover problems worth solving, and create differentiated solutions that new and existing customers will hire over competing alternatives.

There are five key elements to the innovator's playbook:

1. **Business strategy and mission** to set a direction where a company will compete, and how it'll win. In our playbook, we define the strategy using the jobs-to-be-done innovation framework and marketing lens.
2. **Jobs-to-be-done innovation framework** provides the structure and a repeatable process to dive deeply into a customer's problem set. It helps us understand the important jobs people need to get done, their specific desired outcomes and what gets in their way of achieving 100 percent satisfaction.
3. **The design thinker's success triad** to define the innovation game plan. Three core overlapping success elements – desirability, feasibility and viability – must exist for a new product to be a market success.
4. **The business model canvas** to design a business model that delivers consistent value and delight to the targeted market segments. It provides us a simple and clear visualization to successfully address the triad of success criteria

5. **The innovation time horizon map** to focus and manage innovation resources using the right balance of projects: sure bets and game changing new business opportunities. It also provides a technology and marketing capabilities roadmap to execute a strategy that will help us compete successfully in the future.

How to design a winning innovator's playbook

Before we can win the game, we need to define the playing field we choose to compete on and the game we choose to win. Our business strategy should clearly state **"where we compete (the playing field) and how we win the customers' business and loyalty (the game and playbook)."**

Perhaps our current playing field is no longer worth competing on. The game has become too crowded. There's very little differentiation between us and our competitors. For all practical purposes, we're competing primarily on price. That's a race to the bottom and no one wins. This is also known as a "Red Ocean"[24]

Or perhaps the market playing field remains viable, but over time we've become complacent or confused about our direction, or it's become so complicated that it no longer resonates

---

24 Blue Ocean – How to Create Uncontested Market Space and Make the Competition Irrelevant, W. Chan Kim and Renée Mauborgne, Harvard Business School Press, 2005.

Red oceans refer to the known market space – all the industries in existence today. In red oceans, industry boundaries are clearly delineated and accepted, and the competitive rules of the game are known. Companies try to outperform their rivals to grab a greater share of existing demand, usually through marginal changes in offering level and price. As the market space gets crowded, prospects for profits and growth are reduced. Products become commodities, and cut-throat competition turns the red ocean bloody.

with our customers and development team. Too many assumptions are based on yesterday's playbook.

As a result, our team runs on auto pilot cranking out the same old solutions, and stuck in the incremental me-too product doldrums. Customers are beginning to look elsewhere to hire more relevant and promising solutions.

Defining the playing field where we'll win customers and beat competitors

We begin defining our playing field based on current job categories. Then we explore what future jobs our existing job executors (customers) need to get done. We can modify existing job solutions to address new job executors. And we can explore the most challenging and potentially rewarding play in the book - addressing new jobs for new job executors.

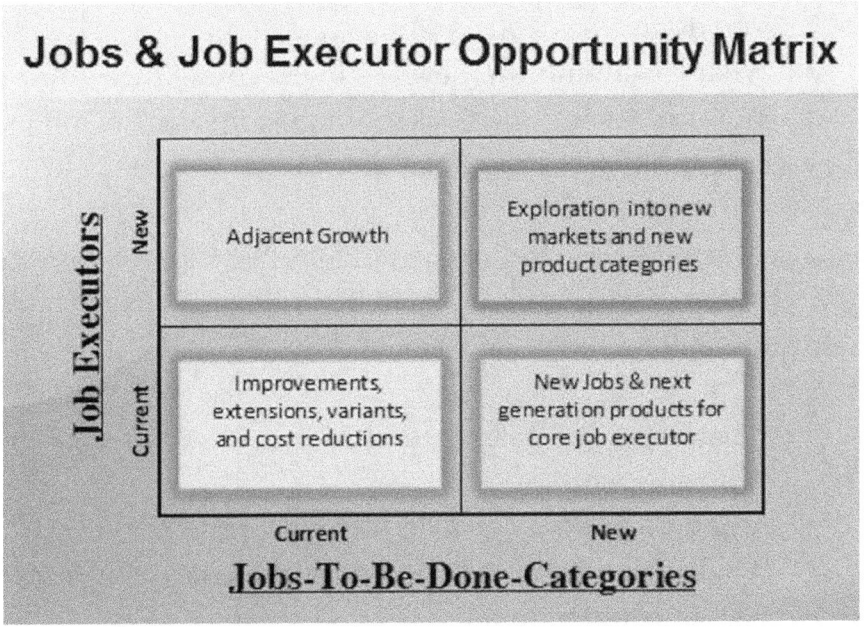

Figure 15.1: Jobs & job executor opportunity matrix.

Even if the current business outlook is good, it's wise to review it periodically and take a different look at business strategy. This requires a new perspective. This time we look at it through the eyes of our current customers (existing job executors), and new customers (potential future job executors). We start by asking:

- Why do customers hire our products and services?
- What outcome are they ultimately trying to achieve?
- What are the jobs they must do to achieve these outcomes?
- What jobs do we help them get done better in achieving these outcomes?
- How much of the job do they get done using our solutions?
- Under what circumstances are they trying to get their jobs done?
- What constraints do they face in executing their jobs?
- How can we improve our solutions to make the job executor's life easier and happier?

Then we look beyond the current jobs. We explore possible new jobs that existing and potential new customers might need help getting done better by asking:

- What other jobs along the job tree are job executors struggling with?
- Are these jobs we can help them get done better?
- What other ancillary jobs are customers trying to do that we could help them get done better?

We continue to identify other potential job executors:

- Who else out there might be trying to do similar jobs but perhaps with different circumstances and desired outcomes?
- If we can identify these groups of job executors, might we be able to adapt our solutions to fit their needs?

The answers to these questions provide a direction that focuses innovation around the important jobs people need to get done.

Playing the game of innovation

We can think of innovation and new product development as a game of moving successfully through what Roger Martin calls **the knowledge funnel**[25].

The knowledge funnel begins with a **Mystery** (a gut feel, for an unexplainable or yet to be validated problem); then it moves to a **Heuristic** (rules of thumb that guide us toward a solution); and ultimately becomes an **Algorithm** (a replicable success formula).

The knowledge funnel is the field the innovation team plays on (see Figure 13.2). The innovation team must traverse a series of phases and decision points to move the concept down the field from mystery to heuristic to algorithm, and achieve commercial success.

---

25 Design of Business: Why Design Thinking is the Next Competitive Advantage, Roger L. Martin, Harvard Business Review Press (October 26, 2009), page 8

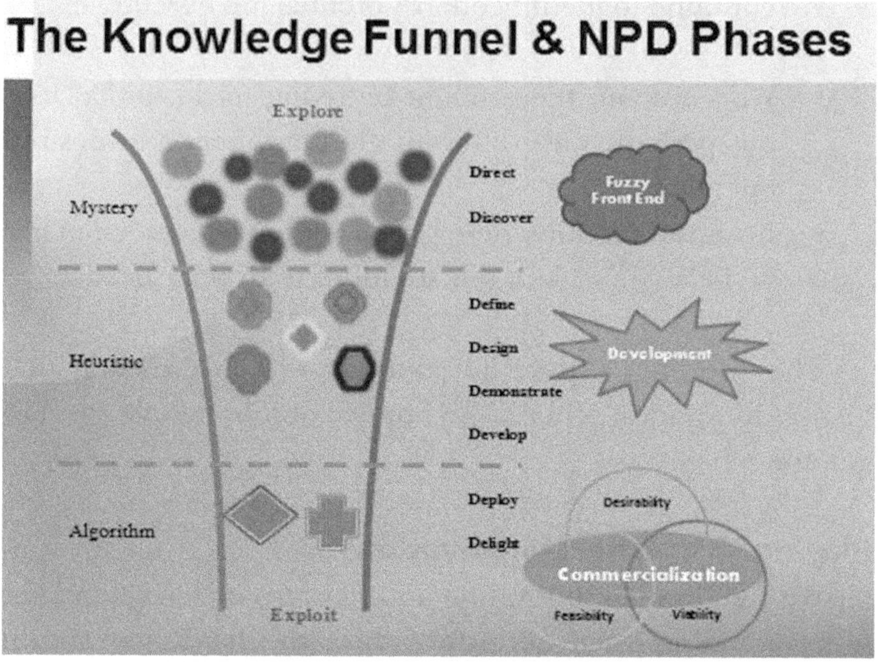

Figure 15.2: *The Knowledge funnel and new product development phases*

Football as a metaphor

Using American football as a metaphor, each phase represents first down markers. And the idea represents the football. When an innovation team makes a first down (achieves a favorable decision point), it can continue to march down the field until it ultimately crosses the goal line (a major product success). Or perhaps an innovation drive ends by kicking a field goal (an incremental success).

Of course there are many challenges in moving the idea across the goal line, including competitors who want to stop us (the defense protecting its goal line). The game throws other challenges at us too, including technical obstacles and marketing challenges.

If we have a robust innovation process, the worst scenario is we shelve the idea (punt the ball) and live for another set of new downs.

The skills of the game

In football, players on a team must learn and master a set of skills to be competitive. Skills include:

- Blocking and tackling
- Running and ball handling
- Forward pass, passing routes and catching
- Kicking and punting
- Reading the defense and offense
- And so forth

Plays are built on the core skills the team collectively masters.

Our innovation team needs to become skilled at executing an innovation system like the jobs-to-be-done innovation framework. It must master the discovery process, the design and development process, the manufacturing process and/or the service creation process, and the marketing and sales process to launch and scale the business.

And like the football quarterback (or coach calling the plays), our innovation team leader must become skilled at deciding what's the best set of plays to move the concept down the knowledge funnel, depending on where the team is in the funnel and the circumstances it faces in making the next move. This is also known as the game strategy.

The "first down" markers and goal line for the innovation team

Once our team has **set** the direction of play, and defined the game it plans to win (attracting and retaining new customers by helping them get important jobs done), we create a game strategy to move through the down markers on the knowledge funnel's grid iron.

Referring to Figure 2 above – the set of down markers (goals and decision points) the team must traverse are:

Discover – Find an opportunity worth pursuing.

Define – Transform the idea into a viable concept.

Design – Understand the problem set and create a solution customers will embrace.

Demonstrate – Validate the design and adapt it as necessary.

Develop – Synthesize the marketing and product requirements into a viable product.

Deploy – Launch the product and scale.

Delight – Continue to deliver value and favorable experiences for the customer.

The game of innovation is not really linear

Though the innovation process has distinct phases, the process isn't linear. As we execute plays in the knowledge funnel, we learn what customers really want, what works technically and what are the realities of the marketing playing field.

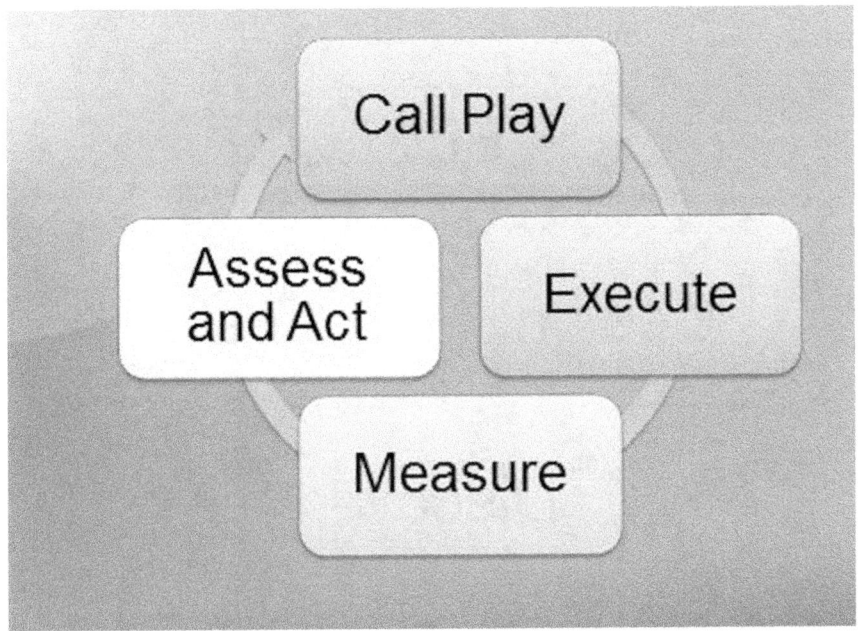

Figure 15.3: *The Learning Loop*

Like the football team, we learn by calling a play, executing the play, measuring the results, and assessing the next set of plays to call to move down the knowledge funnel. More often than not, our game strategy will adapt as our knowledge of the marketing playing field becomes evident.

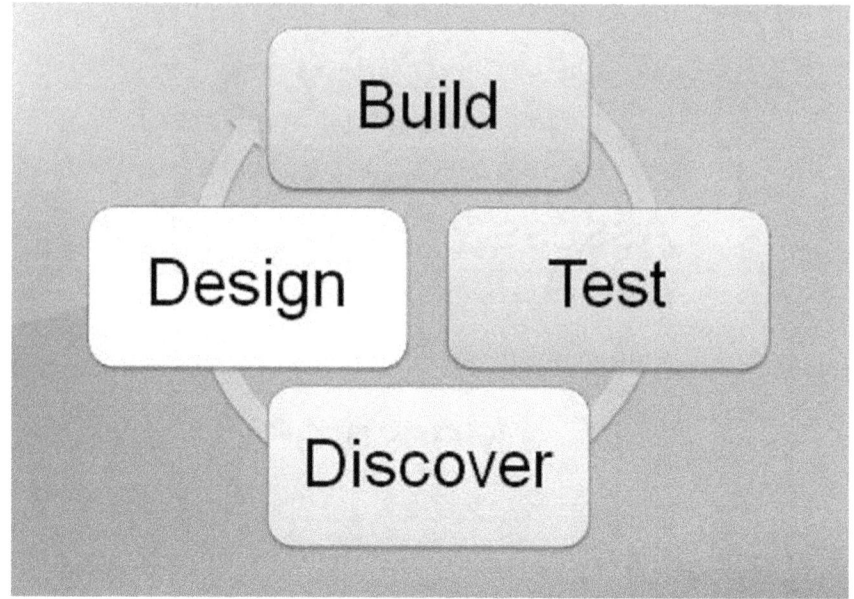

Figure 15.4: Innovation validation loop

And like the football team, not all of our innovation efforts (for a football team, offensive series) will make it through the next decision point. We learn and adapt so we create more powerful concepts that'll make it through the knowledge funnel the next time we take the field in the game of innovation.

The balancing act between desirability, feasibility and viability separates winners from losers

What makes a product successful in the market place? What are the predictable indicators that a concept has the "right stuff" to be a huge success? What are the fundamental criteria that turn promising concepts into winning new products?

In a nutshell: ***all successful new products are found at the overlapping intersection of what design thinkers call the "Triad*** *of Desirability, Feasibility, and Viability*[26]". I call it the **"Design Success Triad."** If any one of these success criteria is missing, the product won't be commercially successful.

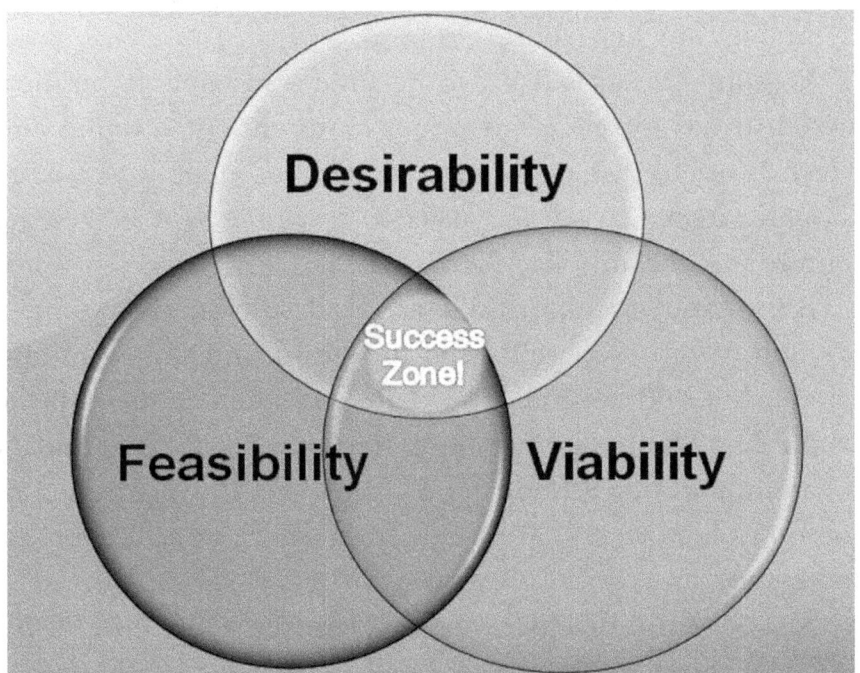

Figure 15.5: *Design success triad*

The "3" criteria of design success

Desirability - The willingness and eagerness of a customer to "hire" the solution once they're aware that the solution exists. Perhaps they weren't even aware that they had the problem, but using the jobs-to-be-done innovation framework and design thinking approach, we can present a solution and story that resonates with potential job executors.

---

26 Change by Design – How Design Thinking Transforms Organizations and Inspires Innovation, Tim Brown, Harper Collins Publishers, 2009

Feasibility - The technical aspect of creating a successful product using the current and near future technical and operational capabilities of a firm and its partners. Everyone wants a Star Trek transporter - but good luck on implementing that technology any time soon.

Viability - What is likely to become a sustainable business model. It has to reach our target customers (marketing and sales). It has to deliver consistent value and delight to a large enough target market at a price-to-cost ratio that makes the venture worth competing for.

If the business opportunity is outside the boundary of any of the three criteria, we'll need to rethink and strategize how we manage the constraints to deliver customer value. Maybe we create a whole new playbook that redefines the boundary constraints to our advantage. This allows us to define a new game (a blue ocean[27]) with new rules where we can compete successfully and win.

All successful products are built on the three criteria for design success. Missing one or more criteria is like missing a leg on a three-legged stool. The stool will fall over. In this case, the product simply won't be commercially viable. Now the question is:

"How do we plan our innovation and development project to make sure, by the end of the development process, all legs of the triad are addressed?"

Here's how:

---

27 Blue Ocean Strategy – How to Create Uncontested Market Space and Make the Competition Irrelevant, W. Chan Kim, Renée Maubourgne, Harvard Business School Press, 2005

The business model canvas as a planning tool

The business model canvas, created by Osterwalder and Pigneur[28] provides a clear approach to early stage strategy and business planning. This is a far more useful tool than a business plan that is often loaded with assumptions and useless information.

Using the business model canvas as our starting point in creating a winning strategy, we can put our best assumptions (our business hypothesis) front and center. We test, hone and adapt our hypothesis as we learn what the market requirements are, so we consistently deliver value at a price and cost that makes the business model viable.

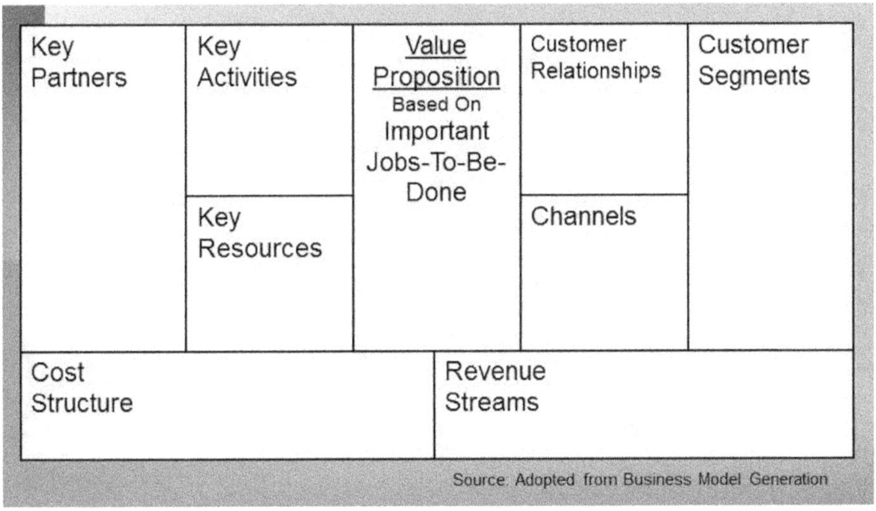

Key Partners	Key Activities	Value Proposition Based On Important Jobs-To-Be-Done	Customer Relationships	Customer Segments
	Key Resources		Channels	
Cost Structure		Revenue Streams		

Source: Adopted from Business Model Generation

Figure 15.6: Business Model Canvas

Mapping the criteria for success onto the business model canvas

---

28 Business Model Generation, Alexander Osterwalder and Yves Pigneur, John Wiley & Sons, Inc., 2010

Each block in the canvas corresponds to one of the criteria.

Desirability – The customer segments (job-executors), the value proposition (important jobs-to-be-done), and the customer relationship (how we treat and interact with our customers).

Feasibility - Key activities, key resources and key partners define our ability to create and produce a winning product.

Viability - The channels to sell and deliver the product and a favorable experience to the customer. The revenue stream – how we make money delivering the product and experience to the customer. And the cost structure – what it'll cost us to deliver the product and experience.

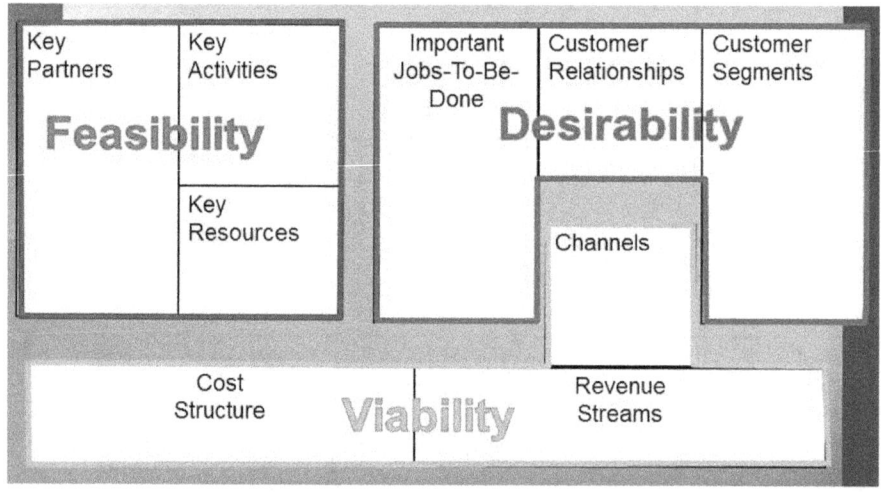

Figure 15.7: Design success triad mapped onto the business model canvas

Using the **Criteria for Success Triad** and the **Business Model Canvas,** we can create our game plan to achieve success in our innovation and new product development endeavors.

Play to win by thinking strategically and planning your strategy time horizons

Innovation and product development are strategic choices a company makes to compete to win. As such we can think of innovation and new product development as applied strategy. Thinking strategically on how to win customers and beat the competition is all about choosing what you will pursue and how you will create the necessary competencies to achieve your aspirations.

Sometimes though, strategic intent (winning through new products and innovation) gets lost in day-to-day activities of making the quarterly numbers. In the pursuit of predictability and "zero defects," companies become too risk adverse and forgo strategic thinking when it comes to defining its new product development road map.

Yes companies need to exploit their current business model. But they also need to be in a constant exploration mode to spot potential future opportunities, while developing the core capabilities and skills to define and create new playing fields, and developing the right players with the right "plays" to take the field and win when the game is on.

It's difficult, if not possible, to predict the future. There are too many variables and "black swans" that will emerge. But one thing I can comfortably predict: ***the future will be played with a new set of rules, and maybe on a totally different playing field.***

Using Strategic Time Horizons to define a balanced portfolio and game plan

The innovation time horizon (see figure15.8) is a visual map to layout the strategy of competing to win into the future. It graphically summarizes the two dimensions of technology and market knowledge. The **"horizon"** analogy relates both to risk and uncertainty, and the time typically required to exploit an opportunity based on the availability of relevant know-how.

As described by Christian Terwiesh and Karl T. Ulrich in their book "Innovation Tournament,"[29] most innovations face two types of uncertainty:

Technology uncertainty describes your ability to execute the opportunity as planned. If the opportunity is based on technology or capability that you have, the level of technological uncertainty is low. It's medium if the technology exist outside your firm, and large if the opportunity is based on new discoveries or advances.

Market uncertainty describes your ability to understand and address the needs of a group of customers. For opportunities that address your existing customers, market uncertainty is low. It's medium for market segments adjacent to your current business but addressed by other firms, and large for markets that are not served by anyone (i.e. the white space).

---

29 "Innovation Tournament, Creating and Selecting Exceptional Opportunities," Christian Terwiesh and Karl T. Ulrich, Harvard Business Review Press (June 9, 2009)

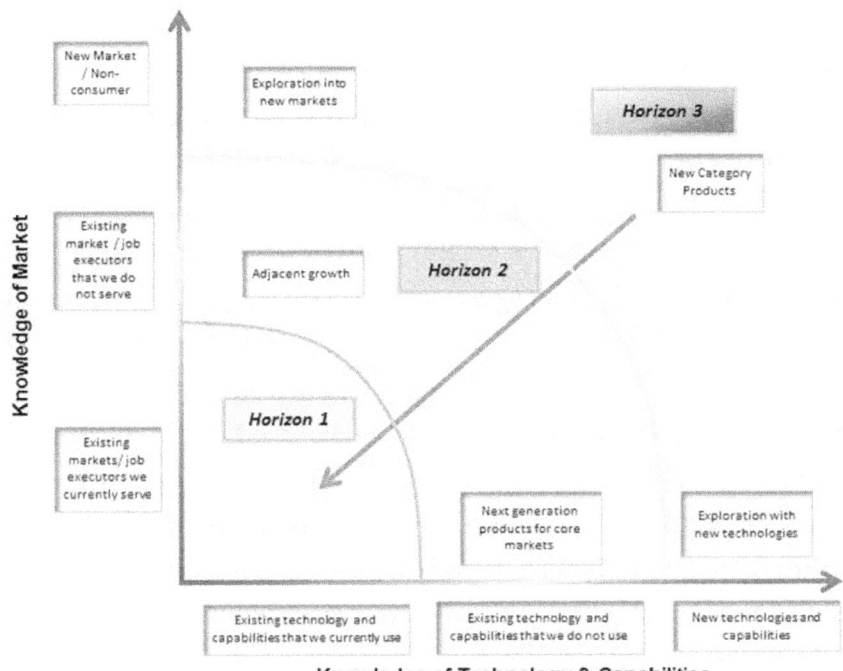

Figure 15.8: Strategic time horizons

Use Strategic Buckets to achieve balance between risk and reward

We can use horizon zones to define the mix of products in your product portfolio to achieve a balance between risk and reward. The percentage of development projects in each bucket is a strategic choice we make. The salient point is that if we don't allocate dedicated resources into horizons 2 and 3, we will eventually become competitively weak and unable to compete with the new rules of the game (or games) as it evolves.

Horizon 1 are the "sure bets" but also represent incremental growth. **Horizon 2** has more upside than Horizon 1 but are still within reach of current knowledge base inside and outside the enterprise. Whereas **horizon 3** has lots of risk but represents potentially breakthrough innovation.

The strategic time horizon map also provides us a visualization of the technologies, capabilities and skills we need to address and master to be competitive on the future's playing fields. The map helps us strategically define and decide what capabilities and resources we need to invest in to field a competitive team.

Managing in the zone

The strategic time horizon map helps us understand where an innovation fits in the knowledge funnel *before deciding the details of the NPD process to develop and commercialize an initial idea.* Each horizon zone should be managed with the right set of processes that specifically address the knowledge gap that exist in each horizon.

Don't forget that the ideation phase needs to be managed with appropriate methods and tools to match the zone under management. Bold new ideas will require bold thinking and discovery based innovation processes. Whereas, incremental improvements are natural progressions in product performance improvements and are more about execution excellence.

By recognizing the ideation processes need to be tailored to match the specific zone characteristics, you will improve your changes of discovering and selecting quality ideas that provide the fuel for future growth within each zone while achieving balance in your project portfolio.

So know your zone and innovate accordingly to come up with the right plays to win the game!

Exercise: Create a business model canvas.

Create a business model canvas for either one of your current product lines or a future product line in the development pipeline. As you create the business model canvas, explore who each section of the canvas affects the three success criteria of the "design thinkers success triad."

Keep your model simple, it's the starting point of building a strategy and will evolve overtime as you discover the market realities and how to win customers and beat the competition.

CHAPTER 16

Final Thoughts:

THE JOBS-TO-BE-DONE INNOVATION framework is a simple and powerful concept: ***people execute jobs to achieve important outcomes.*** And, as Clayton Christensen[30] points out, when they become aware of their important jobs, they will hire (buy) products and services to get those jobs done better, faster and cheaper.

Recall the drill maker from Theodore Levitt's famous line: *"People don't want quarter-inch bits. They want quarter-inch holes."*

If the drill maker only sees his world as making drill bits, he loses focus on the true job to be done - making holes. If the drill maker doesn't probe deeper in understanding the circumstances and problems people face in making holes, he limits his ability to innovate and launch products that customers will value and hire to make holes better, faster and cheaper.

---

30 Clayton M. Christensen is the Kim B. Clark Professor of Business Administration at the Harvard Business School (HBS).

Instead, the drill maker is likely to improve his bits in ways that customers don't value. In the eyes of the customer, the current drill bit may be good enough to get the job done. It doesn't need improving. Thus the customer is unlikely to hire the new drill bit, even though the drill maker believes his new drill is an important improvement.

Taking it a step further, what if the drill maker no longer sees himself as making drill bits, but rather helping customers get important jobs done on the manufacturing line? He may discover quarter inch holes are a means to an end (a sub-job) of bolting two metal parts together in an assembly process.

With his product oriented blinders off, perhaps the drill maker can create a solution that eliminates the job step of making holes by creating a robotic welder to get the assembly job done better, faster and cheaper. But until the drill maker takes his blinders off, he will tend to focus on just being a drill bit maker and miss out on new business opportunities.

The take away about jobs-to-be-done

Drop your product oriented lens and start seeing the world through the jobs-to-be-done lens. When you focus on your products and solutions, you lose touch with the real problems and challenges people face in achieving their ultimate desired outcomes.

You also lose the ability to understand why people are hiring your products in the first place. The reasons may not be obvious; they may be far more important to your customer and lucrative for your firm than you think. To better understand what your customers really want, ask the following questions:

- What are the ultimate desired outcomes people and organizations are trying to accomplish?
- What jobs are they doing to achieve this outcome?
- What gets in the way of achieving 100 percent satisfaction in reaching this outcome?
- What innovations can we create to help them get their important jobs done better, faster and cheaper?

When you shift your thinking in this way, your company will become an innovation engine, creating products and services that'll attract and retain loyal customers, because you help them get important jobs done better than alternative solutions.

The Innovator's Playbook to playing the game of innovation to win

It's my desired outcome that The Innovator's Playbook provides you with an innovation framework for carrying out the necessary upfront discovery and vetting activities that identify problems worth solving, and transforming initial concepts into solutions that customers want and value.

You can now look at problems and opportunities differently - through the eyes of the customer.

As a result of designing and developing your own innovator's playbook, you'll achieve a steady stream of successful new product introductions while avoiding the frustration and waste of launching product duds. And you'll reach a new product development success rate exceeding 60 percent, far outperforming the industry average of 20 percent.[31]

You'll know where you are on the innovation playing field because you've learned the fundamental skills of discovery, design, development, deployment and delighting. You'll play the game and win.

---

31 According to Anthony Ulwick and Clayton Christensen (both are pioneer thought leaders in the jobs-to–be-done innovation framework), companies can improve their success rate from low 20 percent to more than 60 percent, if they use "jobs" and "desired outcomes" as the primary units of analysis.

Suggested Reading List

- **The Innovator's Solution: Creating and Sustaining Successful Growth.** Clayton Christensen and Michael Raynor. Harvard Business Review Press, 2003

- **What Customers Want: Using Outcome-Driven Innovation to Create Breakthrough Products and Services.** Anthony Ulwick. The McGraw-Hill Companies, 2005

- **The Innovator's Guide to Growth: Putting Disruptive Innovation to Work.** Scott D. Anthony, Mark W. Johnson, Joseph V. Sinfield, Elizabeth J. Altman. Harvard Business Review Press, 2008

- **Winning at New Products: Creating Value Through Innovation.** Robert G. Cooper. Basic Books 4th edition, 2011

- **Marketing Malpractice: The Cause and the Cure.** Clayton M. Christensen, Scott Cook, and Taddy Hall. HBR December 2005

- **The Innovator's Dilemma: When New Technologies Cause Great Firms to Fail.** Clayton M. Christensen. Harvard Business Review Press, 2000

- **The Lean Startup: How Today's Entrepreneurs Use Continuous Innovation to Create Radically Successful Businesses.** Eric Ries. Crown Business, 2011

- **Design of Business: Why Design Thinking is the Next Competitive Advantage.** Roger L. Martin. Harvard Business Review Press 2009

- **Blue Ocean – How to Create Uncontested Market Space and Make the Competition Irrelevant.** W. Chan Kim and Renée Mauborgne. Harvard Business School Press, 2005.

- **Change by Design: How Design Thinking Transforms Organizations and Inspires Innovation.** Tim Brown. Harper Collins Publishers, 2009

- **Business Model Generation**. Alexander Osterwalder and Yves Pigneur. John Wiley & Sons, Inc., 2010

About the Author - Kevin B. McGourty

KEVIN B. MCGOURTY is the president of iNPD Center, Inc., where he helps companies develop successful new products and services. He formerly served as VP of Product Planning and Strategy at Varitronic Systems. He is a certified new product development professional and is active in California's innovation and development community. He is the co-author of *Six Steps to the Future: How Mass Customization is Changing Our World.*

Mr. McGourty lives in the Bay Area with his wife, Stephanie, and their two rescue dogs, Freddie and Ginger. He is also a partner in his family wine business, Sea Stone Cellars. He welcomes feedback and can be reached at kmcgourty@inpdcenter.com.